Student housing and the law

Martin Davis and Graham Robson

Student housing and the law
Martin Davis and Graham Robson

ISBN 978 1 903595 77 0

Printed by CPI William Clowes, Beccles NR34 7TL
Typeset by Image Creative Design

Published by Shelter
88 Old Street
London EC1V 9HU
0845 458 4590
www.shelter.org.uk

Everyone should have a home
Shelter, the housing and homelessness charity
Registered charity in England and Wales (263710) and in Scotland (SC002327). RH1925

Supported by ASRA
ASRA promotes and supports the professional activities of individuals working in student accommodation. For more information, visit www.asra.ac.uk

Contents

Introduction

1

Subjects covered in this chapter include...

Student housing: the issues

Types of student accommodation

Providers of student accommodation

Types of letting

Current issues

Student housing: the issues

This book is essentially about the legal issues involved with the renting of accommodation to students. However, the law is only part of the relationship between a student and her/his landlord. Where there is good will on both sides, issues and problems can be resolved by discussion and negotiation. The last thing anyone wants is to go to court. Nevertheless, the law provides a framework for those discussions and a mechanism for resolving problems where there is no other alternative.

The law that affects landlords and tenants has long been regarded as complicated and subject to frequent change. While much of the law applying to student lets is merely the specific application of landlord and tenant law, there are particular issues that affect student lets, not least the fact that a large proportion of lets are made by the university or college where the student is studying. Most educational establishments will provide, or at least arrange, accommodation for first year students. This will be either their own accommodation, or they will have an arrangement with other landlords under which students are guaranteed accommodation in their first year. A smaller number of institutions will provide accommodation for the entire duration of a course, though it's more likely that the student will have to find their own accommodation in later years. In a few places, students may have to find their own place to live from the start.

Students' rights and obligations can be affected by:

- the type of accommodation they live in

- the kind of provider or landlord involved

- the type of letting that is used.

Types of student accommodation

College and university halls of residence

Hall residents almost invariably have their own rooms. Traditionally these rooms, often termed 'study bedrooms', did not contain washing or cooking facilities. Instead these facilities were provided 'communally' with typically one kitchen per floor with a nearby shower/bathroom/toilet 'block'. Older halls are often still of this type. However, newer halls more commonly provide either self contained 'en suite' accommodation, or are organised around a collection of flats each with a bathroom and kitchen. Most modern halls are self-catering, though some still include the provision of meals and other services such as cleaning and the provision of bed linen. Many 'halls' today are really collections of bedsits or small flats with communal facilities but no catering or services. The majority of halls are still run by the college or university but things are changing. In many universities all newer halls are owned and managed by private companies. Unite plc, the largest provider, now claims to have over 35,000 student rooms. This is likely to become ever more common.

Private halls of residence

There is an increasing trend for new halls to be built and run by private companies such as Unite. They may appear to be college halls and may be on land owned by the college, but they are owned and managed by private companies. There is a variety of arrangements but a typical one would be where a college entered into a formal arrangement with a private company under which rents and services are regulated by a long-term agreement with the college. The college determines room allocations but the company manages and maintains the accommodation, and collects the rents.

Accommodation managed by the college

Some private landlords and housing associations lease property to colleges who then sub-lease them to students. The accommodation may be let directly to groups of students or to student families. These are often called **head tenancy** properties. For housing law purposes, these will be treated as let by the university or college.

Living in an owner's home

Some students choose to live with a resident family as a lodger. The student would expect to have their own room or a room shared with another student but may eat with the family and share their facilities. This can work out well if everyone gets on together. Alternatively, the arrangement could involve having a relatively separate existence. In this case, the student may not be so enthusiastic about having to walk past the owner as they come home very late at night. In either case, this is the most insecure form of accommodation and the student can be required to move out with as little as a week's notice (depending on the contract). However, the student can also leave at short notice, which could be useful for someone looking for accommodation elsewhere.

Solo accommodation

Some students living on their own in self-contained accommodation will not share any sleeping, eating, washing or toilet facilities. Others who rent a bedsit – a single room often found in large houses – may have self-contained accommodation with their own cooking facilities, but share bathroom and toilet facilities. Bedsits are overwhelmingly found in the private sector. As long as a student has some self-contained accommodation in a property where the landlord is not living, they are most likely to have an **assured shorthold tenancy**.

Shared accommodation

Many groups of students get together and jointly rent a place from (usually) a private landlord. Sharing with friends can be an attractive idea and is generally a cheaper proposition. In the private sector, these arrangements are likely to be **assured shorthold tenancies** provided the landlord is not living in the same property. The search for accommodation is also easier (and possibly safer) when shared with other people. However, sharing can also create problems and having a manageable number of occupiers is likely to help the situation (see Chapter 6). While shared houses and flats are mainly found in the private sector, they may be available from a university or college, housing associations or (less commonly) local authorities.

Providers of student accommodation

Universities and colleges

Many educational establishments will provide accommodation for students. However, a considerable amount of 'university accommodation' built or refurbished over the last few years is in fact run and managed by private companies. Most, but not necessarily all, universities and colleges, will send accommodation information automatically when offering a place on a course.

Private sector landlords

A large proportion of student lettings are provided by private landlords. While this will clearly cover owner-occupiers and buy-to-let arrangements, it also covers large companies such as Unite who provide rented student accommodation.

Registered social landlords (housing associations)

A small proportion of students may rent property directly from housing associations. As far as housing law is concerned, housing associations fall into a hybrid category, as they are regarded as providers of social housing, but the law about security of tenure that applies has more in common with that used for private landlords. However, as independent non-profit making organisations, housing associations' behaviour has to follow circulars and guidance issued by the Tenants Services Authority (formerly the Housing Corporation).

Local housing authorities

It is fairly unusual for students to be let accommodation by local housing authorities (councils), though council tenants can be students. Where a council letting is made to a person specifically because they are a student, the letting can fall outside the normal 'secure tenancy' arrangement that councils have with their tenants (see Chapter 10).

Types of letting

Non-assured lettings

Virtually all lettings made by universities and colleges fall into this category. This is because they are designated 'specified educational institutions' by the Housing Act 1988. This form of letting would also apply where a student has self-contained accommodation but their private landlord lives in the same house.

Exempt lettings

This specific category would apply where a private landlord not only lives in the same house as the student, but also shares some of the accommodation other than that necessary for means of access. The rights and obligations of the parties will be dependent on the terms of the tenancy agreement (see Chapter 10).

Assured tenancies

Since a change in the law in 1997, an **assured tenancy** has become an uncommon form of letting for private landlords as it now requires a specific 'election' in the tenancy agreement. Even then, it is not possible to have an assured tenancy where the landlord is resident in the same 'dwelling'. Assured tenancies remain a common form of letting for property let by registered social landlords. A student with an assured tenancy will normally be able to continue with a tenancy or extend a let beyond the fixed period even against the wishes of the landlord. The landlord will only be able to recover possession against an unwilling tenant where the tenant has broken the terms of the tenancy agreement, though this is not guaranteed (see Chapter 10).

Assured shorthold tenancies

This is by far the most common form of letting made by private landlords (not housing associations) where the landlord is not resident in the same house. The letting is usually for a fixed period of time though it can run from week to week or month to month. Neither the landlord nor the student can end the letting unilaterally before the period expires, unless the tenant has broken the terms. However, the tenant will not normally be able to continue the tenancy or extend the let beyond the fixed period without the agreement of the landlord.

Licences

Some students living in halls of residence may only have a licence rather than a tenancy. The implications of this are that they have very little security. It isn't always clear whether a licence exists, even where there is an agreement that is headed 'licence' (see Chapter 2).

Current issues

Deposits

Many of the problems that student tenants face occur when they rent from private landlords. These often concern money and the state of the accommodation. A major problem that has been around for many years has been the difficulty of getting a deposit back from a landlord at the end of a tenancy. There can be disputes about whether the tenant has damaged the property, or quite simply the landlord just not returning the deposit. Introduced in April 2007, the **Tenancy Deposit Protection Scheme** now provides a mechanism that involves an independent person deciding whether the deposit should be returned, rather leaving it up to the landlord. It involves either the deposit being held by an independent person rather than the landlord, or the landlord taking out an insurance policy which guarantees to repay the tenant in appropriate cases (see Chapter 3).

Housing conditions

The problem of poor housing conditions or defective services and appliances may also be difficult for a student to deal with. The law is not straightforward here and there is also the risk that making complaints could lead to tension or even eviction. Where a landlord refuses to deal with a problem, low level actions could involve the involvement of a university housing officer. More serious action by the tenant could be based on the contract in the tenancy agreement or on the landlord's duty to keep the accommodation in a safe state of repair. The local authority's environmental health department can step in where the problem involves a statutory nuisance, involves a health hazard, or where the property is (or should be) licensed by the authority. Taking action beyond complaining and negotiating needs some thought. Most students with private landlords will have assured shorthold lets for a fixed period of time. One implication of pursuing a landlord is that s/he may decide not to renew the let after it has expired. Where the letting is on a monthly or weekly basis, the landlord may seek to bring it to an end (see Chapter 10).

Houses in multiple occupation/Licensing

Where students live in a house or flat on a 'multi-occupancy' basis, the accommodation may be what is legally termed 'a house in multiple occupation' (or HMO). A 'typical' HMO is a building consisting of numerous 'bedsits', but multi-occupied private sector accommodation and even 'private' halls may come within the definition.

'Bedsit' HMOs in particular have often been notorious for displaying poor housing standards, and being prone to serious fire and other safety risks. However, until the Housing Act 2004, there was considerable uncertainty as to which properties should be regarded as HMOs, and effective regulation even of properties that were clearly HMOs, was patchy.

There is now a clearer definition of HMOs in place and a comprehensive licensing structure. Most 'multi-occupied' student houses and flats will now be HMOs, although university operated halls are excluded. However, the licensing requirements only apply to larger properties. If they do apply, the building's suitability has to be vetted by the relevant local authority, and the 'management' arrangements (including the manager) have to be satisfactory (see Chapter 3).

The university or college as landlord 2

Subjects covered in this chapter include...

Halls of residence

Students' legal status in halls

What rights does a student have as a non-assured tenant?

The implications of the university's joint role as landlord and provider of education

University regulations and the law

What is the true legal position?

Disciplinary regulations and student housing

Termination of the tenancy/licence agreement

General disciplinary sanctions

Enforcing rent debts and fines by academic sanctions

Eviction

Disciplinary sanctions

Student debts

Halls of residence

When a student considers 'going to university' the image they probably have of their accommodation is of some kind of 'hall of residence' run by the university. Until the 1980s this would have been an accurate image, particularly in the 'old' universities. Even today, in most universities, a significant percentage of first year students live 'in halls' or other university operated accommodation (the alternatives to halls are discussed below). 'Halls' differ considerably in the way they are run. At one extreme (unusual today) there is the fully catered hall often complete with linked services such as the cleaning of rooms and (even) the supply of bed linen. At the other extreme, the 'hall' is really a collection of self-contained flats. Typically in the latter case each flat would have four to six study bedrooms – individually occupied – and the 'flat sharers' would have a kitchen, bathroom and (perhaps) communal area in common. Intermediate examples would involve non-catered arrangements but with individual 'study' bedrooms – perhaps with kitchens and bathrooms on each floor.

Although different types of halls might result in a student having a different legal status, (see below) there are important common features, such as: the halls are normally owned and run by the university, are provided through some kind of accommodation service as an adjunct to the provision of education, and are occupied exclusively by students at the university in question.

Students' legal status in halls

In Chapters 1, 3 and 5, it is suggested that some of those living in halls only have a licence rather than a tenancy. If a student does only have a licence, their legal rights both during and at the end of the agreement period are limited. However, it should not be assumed that all hall occupants are there only as licensees. It is true that most university and college hall agreements use the language of licence rather than tenancy, although they do not necessarily do this consistently. However, as discussed in Chapter 5, the courts have established that the wording in an agreement on such matters may not be conclusive. What ultimately counts is the real nature of the legal relationship. After all, is there exclusive possession in practice? If someone occupies a traditional, fully catered hall, it seems likely that they only have a licence because the university or college will retain control of the premises (and not just the common areas) to enable them to provide the catering, cleaning and other services which the agreement provides for. Although there is no case law specifically on halls of residence, cases on retirement 'homes' (*Abbeyfields (Harpenden) Society Ltd v Woods* (1968)), lodgers (*Huwyler v Ruddy (*1995)) and hotels (*Luganda v Service Hotels Ltd* (1969)) all point to this conclusion.

If someone occupies a 'hall' containing self-contained flats, a finding of 'licence' seems much less likely, whatever the agreement states. As a flat sharer, such a person seems to have exclusive possession, either collectively or individually, and there is nothing in the agreement which requires any real control by the university over the day to day functioning of the accommodation. The university might try to argue that it has special responsibilities to remove anyone misbehaving in a hall because of the need to preserve a proper academic atmosphere, and its obligation to the wider student 'community', all of which should lead to the ordinary rules not applying. A not dissimilar argument worked for a council landlord providing a hostel for vulnerable single males in *Westminster City Council v Clarke* (1992). However, in *Clarke* the vulnerability of the single men, some alcoholics and/or psychologically disturbed, necessitated constant supervision and access. The same can hardly be said for all halls of residence, and 'flat type' halls seem more likely to be viewed as tenancies than licences.

The 'study bedroom with shared communal facilities' arrangement, described above, seems borderline. A lot may depend on how far cooking is allowed in the rooms and how far in other ways they are self contained.

If a student does have a tenancy rather than a licence then it will be a **non-assured** (sometimes called 'common law') **tenancy**. This is because where a landlord is a 'specified educational institution' (which includes all universities and colleges) and the tenant is a student, the tenancy cannot be an **assured** or **assured shorthold**. The relevant law is contained in the Housing

Act 1988, Schedule 1, paragraph 8 and the Assured and
Protected Tenancies (Lettings to Students) Regulations 1998.

What rights does a student have as a non-assured tenant?

While the tenancy agreement is in force, a student is protected
by the covenant of quiet enjoyment (see Chapter 4), and has
exclusive possession (see Chapters 5 and 10). This means that
the college/university does not have unrestricted rights to enter
the flat (see Chapter 4). Moreover, any terms in the tenancy
agreement which conflict with a student's right to exclusive
possession, may be invalid. An example could be if the college/
university tries to control the right to have overnight guests. (For
a more detailed discussion of the rights of **non-assured tenants**
see Chapter 10.)

The final 'status' issue is whether (assuming the student does
have a tenancy) this is a **sole tenancy** or a **joint tenancy**
(see Chapter 5). In most cases, even when a flat is shared,
universities create sole rather than joint agreements, as first
year students in particular will not know each other before
taking up residence and it would be inappropriate to 'group'
them together.

The implications of the university's joint role as landlord and provider of education

Universities, as landlords, are in a unique position. No other
landlord has such clear welfare obligations towards their
tenants, or are more likely to be criticised if things go wrong
with accommodation.

However, no other landlord has the apparent power to control,
or even discipline their tenants via wider university codes
and regulations.

The inter-relationship between the university as landlord and
the university as provider of education is a complicated one
and, at its widest, beyond the scope of this book. However,

given that general university codes and regulations may have a direct bearing on the landlord and tenant relationship between the university and a student tenant, it is necessary to examine the area.

Initially, university codes and regulations are looked at in their general legal context. Then two areas are discussed in detail: disciplinary codes and measures relating to student debt (which can include housing debts). Finally, the Unfair Terms in Consumer Contract Regulations 1999 are discussed.

University regulations and the law

Traditionally, universities have been reluctant to concede that their relationships with their students are governed by ordinary legal principles. They have always argued that by enrolling at university, a student becomes part of an academic community or institution. The rules of this community are, they argue, like the rules of a private club: perhaps challengeable in extreme cases if they deny such basic legal rights as the right to a fair hearing or exhibiting serious bias or bad faith, but generally not. In most cases, universities argue, their students only have recourse to internal appeal and 'dispute resolution' procedures. As a last resort, in many of the old universities, there used to be a final appeal to the University Visitor (traditionally a figure of high standing and social status). The lack of transparency and 'due process' in many of these procedures led to the introduction (by the Higher Education Act 2004) of a statutory scheme for the review of complaints made by students, or former students. The jurisdiction of any surviving Visitor does not extend to matters covered by the legislation.

The current 'designated' independent body for hearing complaints under the scheme is the **Office of the Independent Adjudicator for Higher Education** (OIA). Its statutory role began on 1 January 2005, although it had been established on a voluntary basis from 29 March 2004. The OIA's remit is to consider, among other things, complaints about 'a service provided…by a Higher Education Institution'. In theory, this could include complaints about a university's housing 'services'. For further information, see www.oiahe.org.uk

Despite the establishment of this more 'legalistic' framework for the resolution of student disputes, many 'old' universities in particular are still very reluctant to admit that the ordinary law has a part to play in their relationships with their students. The main argument used is that the university is a chartered corporation and that students, like university staff, are all members of the corporation. 'Arms length' contractual arrangements are, they argue, both legally and practically inappropriate. This is, at root, a variation on the argument already discussed that everyone is a member of the same 'club'.

What is the true legal position?

There may be a distinction between the position of many of the 'old' universities and the position of the 'new' ones ('new' universities are those which have come into being since 1992 – mainly ex-polytechnics). None of the latter had Visitors, nor do they have chartered corporation status. There seems little doubt that the relationship between a 'new' university and its students is a contractual one. The courts may be reluctant to interfere with exercise by the university of pure academic judgment. However, disciplinary codes, descriptions of course and module details, and even matters relating to the award or withholding of qualifications, all seem to be part of the general 'contract of study' between the university and its students. Where the university role as academic provider and provider of accommodation intersect, it seems inevitable that the relevant rules and regulations have a contractual basis.

As regards those 'old' universities which are chartered corporations and which have a Visitor, there may be a little more doubt. In the recent case of *Clark v University of Lincolnshire and Humberside* (2000) the Court of Appeal seemed to say that a contractual claim against an essentially public body, such as a chartered university, was generally inappropriate (the opposite was thought to be true for 'new' universities). This conclusion however, was not necessary for the decision in the case itself and will not necessarily be followed in future cases.

If a student is considering a contractual claim against an 'old' chartered university, they should be prepared for a long, drawn out struggle. Invoking internal complaints procedures, and (potentially) the OIA will often be an easier option.

It is well established that even a chartered university is bound by public law principles and is potentially subject to its actions being 'judicially reviewed'. If it is felt that in applying its rules, the university has been guilty of bias, has disciplinary rules which prevent impartiality, or generally has behaved highly unreasonably, there may be some mileage in a 'public law' challenge.

It may also be possible to invoke the Human Rights Act 1998 in suitable cases. It seems likely that a university is either a public body or carrying out a public function so can therefore potentially 'trigger' the Act.

Taking a case to the high court is a lengthy business even if **public funding** (formerly known as legal aid) is available. Initially recourse to internal complaints procedures and the OIA seems likely in most cases to be a more 'profitable' route.

Regardless of whatever the legal relationship between a university and its students is when it is fulfilling its role as a provider of education, in its role as landlord, the relationship is a contractual one. As in any other tenancy (or licence) agreement, there will be various clauses concerning matters such as 'misbehaviour' by the tenants/licensees and non-payment of the rent or licence charge. What is unique about the position of the university landlord is that their tenancy/licence agreements (particularly those concerning halls of residence) are normally interlinked with the general disciplinary codes and regulations of the university. Moreover the university is also in a unique position in that it is able to control non-payment of rent and licence fees by treating them as general debts owing to the university with the consequent sanctions attached to such debts.

Disciplinary regulations and student housing

Almost invariably, tenancy and licence agreements used by universities concerning halls of residence contain a clause that the disciplinary rules and procedures of the university apply to actions carried out by students while in halls. A typical clause might be 'The university disciplinary rules and procedures apply to this agreement'. Typical 'misbehaviour' covered might be excessive noise, vandalism (including 'pranks' such as letting off fire extinguishers) and harassment of other students (including sexual and racial harassment).

Two different types of result can follow from any such student 'misbehaviour':

- The tenancy/licence agreement may further provide that any, or some specified breach(s) of the disciplinary regulations will lead to the termination of the agreement (either automatically or in specified circumstances).

- The general sanctions in the disciplinary regulations will 'kick in' – typically ranging from fines, to either suspension, or even expulsion from, the university.

From a university perspective, it is certainly better to incorporate reference to the disciplinary codes in the tenancy/licence agreement. If this does not happen but (instead) reliance is placed on the code itself referring back to halls or other university accommodation, there may be issues as to whether the code was given to students too late (this is typically after the hall agreement has been signed). In general terms, the law states that for a contractual term to be legally binding, it needs either to be in a signed agreement or reasonable notice of it has to be given before the contract is finalised.

Termination of the tenancy/licence agreement

If a tenancy/licence agreement is periodic (see Chapter 5), then a notice to quit of a minimum four weeks' duration is needed to bring it to an end (see Chapter 10). No further reasons need to be given by the university since even if it is a tenancy, it will be a non-assured 'exempt' one because of the Housing Act 1988, Schedule 1, paragraph 8 and the Assured and Protected Tenancies (Letting to Students) Regulations 1998. However, a court order will be needed if a student refuses to leave on expiry of the notice to quit.

The need for a court order is not always appreciated by universities. Any student 'falling foul' of a clause requiring them to leave halls or other university-owned accommodation, should be advised to seek legal advice immediately. If the university tries to evict them without a court order, it may be guilty of unlawful eviction (see Chapter 4).

If the agreement is for a fixed term (see Chapter 5) such as a university term or the academic year, there is no need for a notice to quit (see Chapter 10). However, if the university intends to terminate the agreement before the end of its normal duration, there will need to be a 'break' clause in the contract. If the intention is to terminate the agreement because of a breach of disciplinary regulations or other matters such as non-payment of rent, there will need to be express reference to this in the 'break' clause. A court order will, again, be needed if the student refuses to leave.

A controversial point concerning fixed-term agreements (whether tenancies or licences) is the effect of the Unfair Terms in Consumer Contracts Regulations 1999 (discussed later). No particular reason for seeking possession as such needs to be shown in relation to an 'exempt' university/student tenancy, nor as regards a licence. However, if the university attempts to terminate the tenancy/licence before the normal term expires, it will only be able to do so if the agreement states it has such a right, and spells out the circumstances where this right can be exercised. Arguably if the reasons given (whether linked to disciplinary codes or not) are 'unfair', they may be unenforceable. The point is, as yet, untested (although paragraph 3.61 of the Office of Fair Trading (OFT) Guide does state that the OFT would challenge any term stating or implying that a tenant could be evicted at any time, simply at a landlord's discretion) and advice should always be sought concerning it. (For a general discussion of the Unfair Terms Regulations, see Chapter 5.)

General disciplinary sanctions

The issues raised earlier about the legal status of disciplinary codes apply directly here. On the assumption that the codes have a contractual basis, their enforceability must now be subject to the Unfair Terms in Consumer Contracts Regulations 1999. If, particularly in the case of chartered 'old' universities, their status is more akin to the rules of a club or learned society, they may only be challengeable on a public law basis.

The distinction could be important. If the rules are effectively contractual terms, they are probably now subject to a general requirement of fairness (see Chapter 5), whereas if the only legal controls are public law ones, in most cases the rules themselves will not be directly challengeable, although their application must be unbiased and operate in an impartial manner.

The following are common regulations likely to arise when you live in a hall of residence:

- seeking to impose 'collective responsibility' for damage and vandalism in the hall by way of 'fining' all students in the particular section of the hall irrespective of proof of direct responsibility

- imposing fines for being noisy or drunk in hall.

If the basis of the above clauses is contractual (ie they form part of an agreement to study between the university and its students), then issues of fairness under the 1999 regulations arise. Certainly the OFT has already required deletion of terms in student tenancy agreements which imposed blanket 'collective responsibility' for damage/undue wear and tear. However if their basis is a public law one, challenge under the regulations would not be possible. If the disciplinary code is directly incorporated into the hall agreement (which is certainly contractual), the regulations should apply.

Case

At 3am, university security received a complaint from Victoria and Melanie in Flat 1 that they were being disturbed by noise from a neighbouring flat and intimidated by Robbie, Giles and Ronan when they went to complain. The security officers entered the flat using a passkey and knocked on the bedroom door several times but there was no reply. It was thought that the music was so loud that the students could not hear. The officers entered the room and one of them introduced himself. He was immediately subjected to verbal abuse. The three occupants of the room refused to identify themselves and stated that they believed they had the right to do what they wanted, as they were paying to live there. The security officers left and reported the matter to the residences manager the next day.

A disciplinary hearing was held with Robbie, the official occupant of the room, who was held responsible for the actions of his guests. He was found to be in breach of his tenancy agreement and four of the house rules, which comprised part of the tenancy agreement. A fine of £70 was imposed, along with a final written warning.

Comment

Although this may appear to be a fairly common scenario, it is unclear whether the university acted within its powers. University staff can only enter students' premises if either the students are licensees, or if the letting agreement specifically covers this point. There is also the issue of the appropriateness of fines in the contract: no private landlord would be able to fine a student.

Enforcing rent debts and fines by academic sanctions

It is extremely common for universities to provide in both their disciplinary codes and in their general academic regulations, that if a student has any outstanding fines or other debts with the university at the end of an academic year, s/he is not allowed to progress on to the next year of their course or to receive an Award Certificate. It is normally provided (or at least assumed by the university) that outstanding rent (whether from hall or head tenancy accommodation) is a debt for this purpose. In a few cases, the relevant regulations even prohibit graduation. It may also be that some universities still withhold examination results from students until all debts are paid.

A number of issues arise here:

* It is possible that withholding results and/or degree certification by the university might be a breach of the Human Rights Act 1998.

* If the university continues to withhold results in these circumstances, this seems to be in breach of the Data Protection Act 1988. Most universities have now accepted this.

* A 'blanket'/automatic denial of 'progression' or graduation, however small the debt, is likely to be a breach of the Unfair Terms in Consumer Contracts Regulations 1999. Such a clause seems excessively one-sided and imbalanced. (The regulations are discussed in detail in Chapter 5.)

Arguably, to threaten such sanctions could be a breach of section 40 of the Administration of Justice Act 1970 which makes it an offence for a creditor to harass their debtors by excessive or unreasonable demands. Rent or licence charges may, for example, be in arrears because of a dispute over disrepair or the non-provision of services (see Chapter 8). To (in effect) coerce a reluctant student into paying by threatening to withhold their degree is, arguably, harassment. It is certainly the exercise of 'one-sided' power and no other landlord is in a similar position concerning the non-payment of rent or licence charges. **Please note**, this point has not been tested in the courts and further legal advice should always be sought concerning it.

Case

At University A, students are given written information about the university's halls of residence. In the document, it says:

'Any outstanding hall rent is treated as a debt to the university and students in debt may be withdrawn from their course or, where appropriate, have their award withheld'.

When students fill in their application form for a place in hall, they sign that they have read and understood this. The tenancy agreement issued makes no reference to this clause.

The university's academic regulations state that:

'Where a student has not yet fulfilled a legitimate requirement of the university, including, inter alia, the settlement of any outstanding debt to the university, or to a partner institution at which the student has studied as part of their course scheme at the university, the Academic Registrar may withhold from the student any academic award conferred by the university and s/he shall not be entitled to confirmation of his/her result'.

In the past, the university has withheld defaulting students' results but, in practice, it appears that the university was reluctant to hold back results and awards unless the circumstances were very clear and there was a substantial debt.

It seems that the policy has not been enforced at all for the last couple of years, but there has been no publicly stated change of practice or policy.

Comment

It appears that the university has either successfully incorporated the penalty clause into the tenancy agreement or has set up a pre-tenancy collateral contract. However, the academic regulation is very sweeping in its scope and insufficiently targeted. It is not clear whether the debts referred to relate to the payment of course fees, library fines or the costs of renting college accommodation. As a result, they may be susceptible to challenge.

Eviction

All occupants of university owned or 'head tenancy' accommodation will either be licensees or have non-assured 'exempt' tenancies. If the agreement is a 'periodic' one (see Chapter 5), no reason has to be given to terminate it, and only a four week notice to quit needs to be given, although a court order is required (see Chapter 10). Therefore even if a stated reason in the contract is unenforceable as 'unfair' in principle, this makes no difference to the university's right to evict if it wishes to.

However, if the agreement is for a fixed period (either an academic term or the whole academic year in most cases, and this is the norm in halls of residence and very common for other residential agreements) the position may be different. Before a university can evict, it needs to 'break' the fixed-term agreement before its normal expiry date. An unrestricted right to do so would almost certainly be unfair under the regulations. Even a right to do so for specific reasons may be unfair if either the stated reasons are too wide (for example, a general right to terminate the agreement for 'causing nuisance' or 'excessive noise'), or too trivial when compared to the severe sanction of eviction. Of course, serious and specific nuisances or rent arrears may well justify eviction, but a clause which has potentially unfair consequences may well be void even if it can be used quite fairly.

As stated earlier, the law here is untested but it is the view of the authors that universities should re-examine their fixed-term residential agreements to ensure that 'eviction' clauses are as clearly worded, even-handed and proportionate as possible.

Disciplinary sanctions

As discussed above, typical sanctions for 'misbehaviour' in halls range from fines, to suspension or expulsion from university. The point about inadequate notice of terms amounting to potential unfairness is particularly significant here. It is doubtful whether a 'blanket' clause such as 'The university's regulations and disciplinary code of conduct apply to this agreement and the student is taken to have read and understood these regulations before signing this agreement' will suffice. At the very least, the licence/tenancy agreement itself should spell out in clear and straightforward language what 'misbehaviour' in halls is covered by the disciplinary code and what the potential sanctions are.

As regards the substance of any sanctions imposed, the old saying that the 'punishment should fit the crime' seems relevant. Suspension or even expulsion from the university for (say) a severe case of sexual or racial harassment may be entirely appropriate and 'fair'. Fines for minor damage or vandalism may be another matter. No other landlord/licensor has the power to impose a fine on her/his tenants/licensees – instead other legal steps have to be taken to recover compensation.

Further issues arise concerning 'collective responsibility' clauses, for example holding a whole block or corridor of a hall liable for damage caused in that area irrespective of proof of responsibility. This seems very hard to justify as a fair and balanced clause (certainly if imposed automatically without prior recourse to internal review and mediation). As already mentioned, the OFT appears to take the same view.

If 'misbehaviour' in halls triggers the severe punishment of eviction from halls, questions may be asked whether it is fair to impose additional sanctions on top of this.

Student debts

Normally a landlord has to pursue outstanding rent claims against a student through the courts. This may be time consuming and irritating but is part of the normal legal process. It must be in doubt how fair it is for a university to reserve for itself the sanction of withholding qualifications or blocking progression on to the next year of a course on the basis that rent outstanding is a debt owed to the university and that any debt justifies serious sanctions. The sum involved may be small, or may even be in dispute. This seems a very clear example of (to use the words of regulation 5 of the Unfair Terms in Consumer Contracts Regulations 1999) a 'significant imbalance in the party's rights and obligations...to the detriment [of the] student'.

Universities should consider more focused and targeted debt recovery clauses, perhaps reserving the penalty of academic sanctions for serious debts which have been fully investigated and where attempts at internal arbitration or mediation have been made without success.

Issues to be organised before renting

3

Subjects covered in this chapter include...

Does the landlord have permission to let?

Licensing of houses in multiple occupation

Management orders

Overcrowding notices

The Tenancy Deposit Protection Scheme

Safety issues

Insurance for landlords

Insurance for tenants

Accreditation schemes

Introduction

Many, if not most, landlords tend to think that a house or flat is 'theirs', not only in the obvious sense that they are the owner, but also in that they have an absolute right to use any particular form of contract they like, impose whatever terms they wish on their tenants, and come and go as they please in the property. This is a wholly misguided view. Later chapters will demonstrate the extent of the legal controls and constraints on landlords concerning access to 'their' property, the terms they can impose, and the standards of repair that have to be maintained.

However, there are a number of fundamental issues that need to be considered before a house or flat is rented. Some of these (for example issues relating to gas and electrical standards and fire safety) have been an important part of the law for some time. Others (in particular, issues concerning licensing and the tenancy deposit scheme) are new. Landlords and tenants need to be aware of these legal controls before a tenancy agreement is signed, or any money changes hands. This may be an issue (for a tenant) of personal safety and security, it may be an issue for a landlord of losing significant control over 'repossession' of the property because of a failure to comply with licensing or tenancy deposit provisions, or it may, simply but crucially, be a question of money.

The law in this chapter generally applies to all landlords and tenants, and not merely to student tenancies. However, the transient nature of many student 'lets', and the inexperience of both students and many of their landlords, is likely to make the law particularly important in relation to student tenancies.

Does the landlord have permission to let?

This can be important in a number of situations:

- where the landlord has a mortgage on the property
- where the landlord is a tenant themselves
- in relation to insurances on the property.

It should be noted that even if a tenancy is granted without the consent of the lender/head landlord, it is still binding on the immediate landlord, and the tenant will continue to enjoy their rights/obligations against her/him. The immediate landlord cannot end the tenancy simply because the lender/head landlord has become aware of the student tenancy. The issue is as to what rights/security, if any, the student tenant will have if the lender/head landlord takes possession action against the immediate landlord.

Where the landlord has a mortgage, there are two connected issues:

- whether the (student) tenancy was created prior to the mortgage
- whether the landlord/borrower has permission to let from the lender.

If the tenancy predates the landlord's mortgage, there is no problem. Usually, the mortgage predates the tenancy and if the tenancy was granted without consent, the tenant will have no defence if the lender takes possession action. Most mortgage agreements prohibit a borrower from granting tenancies. Certain lenders do allow borrowers to grant mortgages – buy-to-let mortgages being the obvious example. There is some uncertainty about the tenant's status in the event that the mortgage predates the tenancy and the tenancy was granted with consent. The law here is complex and further advice should always be sought.

If there isn't any consent, and the tenancy was only granted after the mortgage, the lender may be able to repossess and so evict the tenant even if the latter knew nothing of the mortgage. Technically damages can be sought from the landlord in such a case. Again, advice should always be sought.

Where the landlord is a tenant themselves, it depends on whether the landlord had permission to sublet. If not, the 'head' landlord may decide to take possession proceedings that again puts the student tenant in a vulnerable position (although such a 'breach of covenant' by the landlord is only a discretionary ground for possession).

If there is no permission to let, the landlord's insurance may be rendered void in the event of a claim (see Chapter 4).

Licensing of houses in multiple occupation

Landlords of some types of flats and houses in multiple occupation (or HMOs as they are usually referred to) must obtain a licence from the local authority to rent them out.

HMOs have always displayed distinct and difficult issues. Notoriously, they display some of the worst standards, are prone to serious fire and other safety risks, and are prone to overbearing, intrusive and sometimes harassing landlord behaviour.Coupled with these problems is the fact that many of the occupants of HMOs are vulnerable to exploitation because of their age and economic insecurity. The need to closely regulate HMOs was increasingly recognised and new standards, including wide ranging licensing provisions, were introduced by the Housing Act 2004.

What is an HMO?

The idea, as the name suggests, is that of a building or part of a building in 'multiple' rather than 'single' occupation ('single' in the sense of one 'household' occupying). The Housing Act 2004, section 254 sets out a number of tests for determining whether something is an HMO. In addition, some of the key criteria require further definition – in particular the idea of being a member of the same 'household' as someone else. Finally, some properties which would otherwise be HMOs are specifically excluded. Although the legislation appears to create three distinct 'tests' to establish an HMO (the 'standard' test, the self contained flat test, and the converted building test), certain key criteria applies 'across the board':

* The living accommodation in the building/flat must be occupied by individuals who are not part of the same 'household' (this is discussed in more detail below).

* The individuals concerned must occupy the building/flat as their 'only or main residence'. The Housing Act 2004, section 259 deems certain individuals to be occupying accommodation as their 'only or main residence'. Crucially for the purpose of this book all those who occupy the building/flat for the purpose of full-time study

in further education/higher education are deemed
to be occupying it as their 'only or main residence'.

- 'Living accommodation' must be the 'sole use' that
  the building/flat is being put to.

- Some 'consideration' (most obviously rent) is being
  paid for the right to occupy the building/flat.

- Two (or more) households share at least one basic
  amenity, or the living accommodation is lacking one
  or more basic amenity. 'Basic amenities' mean a toilet,
  personal washing facilities and cooking facilities.

Membership of the same household

This is a complex concept which proved very hard to 'pin
down' under the law prior to the Housing Act 2004 (HA 2004),
leading to numerous appeals to the courts from local authorities
attempting to apply provisions relating to HMOs (see for
example *Barnes v Sheffield City Council* (1995) *and Rogers v
Islington London Borough Council* (1999)).

The issue has proved to be particularly acute in relation to
students who may occupy buildings/flats in ways which do
not precisely model conventional 'family' structures. In the
past, everything relied on whether those occupying a building/
flat saw themselves as, and acted in ways to demonstrate that
they were, a single 'group' or not. The new law makes things
clearer and simpler, even though no attempt has been made
in the HA 2004 to provide any general/overall definition of a
'household'. Instead (in section 258) the legislation specifies
the circumstances in which a group of people do not form a
single household. Generally, the following people will only be
classed as being part of the same 'household' as:

- relatives (parents, grandparents, siblings, aunts, uncles,
  nephews, nieces, cousins, children and grandchildren)

- partners (if any) – married, unmarried, or civil partnerships

- domestic employees, eg au pairs

- carers in some situations

- foster children/parents in some situations.

This suggests that a group of students living together in a house or flat will not generally be seen as a single household, however close, 'collective' and 'communal'. From this, it can be assumed that most 'multi-occupied' private sector student accommodation will now, in principle come within the new HMO licensing controls, assuming that the property is one generally requiring licensing (see below).

Exceptions from the definition of an HMO

Such exceptions are contained in HA 2004, Schedule 14. The most significant exceptions seem to be:

* a building/part of a building which is 'controlled or managed' by a public sector body, for example, a local housing authority or housing association

* a building/part of a building occupied by a person/ persons who own that building/part of a building, together with members of their household and no more than two others (for example two lodgers)

* a building/part of a building occupied 'solely or principally by persons who occupy it for the purpose of undertaking a full-time course of further education/higher education and where the body managing/controlling the building is the academic institution at which the person is studying'.

The last exception is the key one for students. Subjecting university run student housing to mandatory licensing was not considered necessary as such accommodation was considered to be responsibly managed by semi-public bodies. A list of appropriate 'educational establishments' (155 in total) falling outside licensing requirements is now provided in the Houses in Multiple Occupation (Specified Educational Establishments) (England) Regulations 2006. There are, as an alternative, Codes of Practice concerning appropriate standards in university operated accommodation. After some discussion, 'commercial' landlords who provide student accommodation on a large scale are still subject to HMO licensing in principle, even if they have 'signed up' to the same Codes of Practice as universities. However, it is equally clear that they will receive more 'relaxed' and favourable treatment including reduced licence fees.

Must the HMO be licensed?

Whether an HMO must be licensed, depends on the size/scale of the HMO. If it is not excluded (as discussed above), an HMO must be licensed if it has **three or more storeys,** occupied by **five or more people** and **containing two or more households.** 'Storey' has a broad definition, including attics and basements (but not 'mezzanine' floors used solely as a means of access).

A local authority has discretion to introduce a licensing scheme for other HMOs, but this will depend entirely on local conditions and policies.

Obligations on landlords

Many landlords of HMOs are not currently licensed – in part because some local authorities are still operating transitional schemes, or have not processed their applications. However, in theory all landlords of HMOs that require licensing must:

- be licensed

- have made an application for a licence which has not yet been granted or refused

- have notified the local authority that they intend to take steps to ensure that an HMO is no longer required to be licensed (eg reducing the number of occupants) – in which case the local authority may issue a **temporary exemption notice** – initially for three months, but extendable up to six months.

In terms of the above there is an obvious temptation for a landlord to try to evict tenants, so as to take the building/part of a building outside licensing. In such a case, it is highly arguable that the 'health, safety and welfare' of those affected is threatened which would require the local authority to make an **interim management order** permitting the authority to take over the management of the building (Housing Act 2004, sections 102 and 104). In practice, this power is most likely to be invoked where the evictions are unlawful, or harassment is involved (see Chapter 4), but the power is not limited to such cases.

Granting/refusal of licences

In considering whether to grant a licence or not, a local authority must consider:

- that the building/part of a building is reasonably suitable for occupation by not more than the maximum number of occupants/households specified in the application (or can be made suitable by the imposition of conditions)

- that the proposed licence holder is a 'fit and proper person' to be the licence holder

- that the proposed manager is a 'fit and proper person' to be the manager

- that the proposed management arrangements for the house are otherwise satisfactory.

'Suitability' relates to minimum standards concerning toilets, bathrooms, kitchens, etc. Broadly, there needs to be a separate toilet/bathroom for every five sharing occupiers, and a kitchen that 'adequately enables' [the] stor[ing], prepar[ing] and cook[ing] of food'. (For full details, see Schedule 3 of the Licensing and Management of Houses in Multiple Occupation (Miscellaneous Provisions) (England) Regulations 2006.) The criteria for deciding if someone is a 'fit and proper' person are whether (or not) the person in question has unspent convictions for offences involving fraud, dishonesty, violence, drugs or sexual malpractice; has been guilty of unlawful discrimination of the grounds of sex, colour, race or disability; or has had civil judgments made against her/him concerning housing, environmental health or landlord and tenant law. The last 'category' potentially encompasses landlords unlawfully retaining deposits, or having damage disrepair claims made against them (see Chapter 8), as well as those 'guilty' of matters such as harassment and unlawful eviction.

Licences may be granted subject to conditions such as the carrying out of works of improvement on the property, or prohibition of the use of certain parts of the property.

A licence must include the following conditions:

- smoke alarms must be fitted and kept in proper working order

- if gas is supplied to the property, the licence holder must produce a gas safety certificate issued within the last 12 months

- a declaration of safety as regards electrical appliances and furniture must be supplied to the local authority

- the occupiers of the property must be supplied with a written statement of the terms on which they occupy it.

Consequences of an HMO requiring licensing remaining unlicensed

There are three main consequences, two of which directly involve a tenant's civil rights. In the first two consequences, there is no sanction if there is an ongoing appeal. An HMO landlord is 'excused' if there is an ongoing appeal concerning any refusal by the authority of a licence or a temporary exemption certificate.

Failure to have a required licence is a criminal offence. It is also an offence to breach licence conditions (eg as to the maximum number of occupants in an HMO). Offences are committed by any person having control or managing an HMO.

Rent Repayment Orders

a) Local authority application

Where a landlord has been convicted of an offence (as above) the local authority may apply to a Residential Property Tribunal (RPT) for an order that any housing benefit (HB) shall be repaid to the authority – this is a Rent Repayment Order (RPO). This may be of limited interest to most student tenants, given the general non-availability of HB to students (see Chapter 7). Even where HB is payable, an RPO does not directly benefit the student.

b) Occupiers application

Any occupier has 12 months from the date of a conviction (or local authority declaration that an offence has been committed) to apply to an RPT for an order that all rent paid to the landlord, while the landlord was guilty of an offence, should be repaid to her/him. This is, of course, a potentially valuable right and a serious disincentive for landlords not to be licensed, but it does depend initially on the local authority having decided to prosecute/issue a declaration. If this has not happened, a tenant might realistically anticipate a large sum of rent to be repayable to them at some future date but have no defence in the short term to a possession action brought on account of rent arrears (see Chapter 10).

Restrictions on terminating a tenancy

If an HMO required to be licensed remains unlicensed, any **section 21 possession notice** required as an initial step in terminating an **assured shorthold tenancy** (ASTs) (see Chapter 10) is invalid. This is likely to be a serious deterrent to 'private' landlords of students who operate HMOs since their tenancies are almost invariably likely to be ASTs.

Management orders

Further provisions, in the form of management orders, exist, to control HMO's that require licensing, but are unlikely to fulfil licence conditions. There are two main types of management orders likely to affect student properties:

Interim Management Orders (IMOs) (Housing Act 2004, sections 102–114) – an IMO transfers the management of a property to the relevant local housing authority for a period of up to 12 months. Such an order allows the authority to take possession, carry out repairs and collect rents. The authority must repay the landlord any surplus of income over expenditure.

An authority must take IMO enforcement action concerning a licensable property if:

- there is no realistic prospect of it granting a licence in the near future (this does not apply if a temporary exemption certificate is in force); or

- to protect the health and safety of those in the property or others in the vicinity of it.

Additionally, an authority should take IMO action if it has revoked a licence and considers that it is unlikely that a licence will be reissued in the near future, or that the 'health and safety condition' is satisfied.

An authority can apply to an RPT to authorise an IMO concerning a non-licensable property if there is a health and safety risk. If a landlord wants to appeal against an IMO, s/he must do so via an RPT.

Final Management Orders (FMOs) (Housing Act 2004, sections 113–122) – an FMO is only possible where an IMO, or another FMO was in force immediately beforehand. Other than FMOs lasting for five years, the conditions are much the same as regards IMOs. When an FMO is issued, an authority has to also produce a management scheme for the property, covering areas such as the amount of rent it will seek to obtain and any works they propose to carry out. Landlords can appeal to RPT's in the same way as concerning IMOs.

Overcrowding notices

In granting a licence for an HMO, an authority must set, as a condition of the licence, the maximum number of tenants that can occupy the property.

An authority can regulate levels of occupancy in HMOs which are not required to be licensed by using **overcrowding notices** (Housing Act 2004, sections 139–144). Such a notice can be served where the authority considers that an excessive number of people are being accommodated in, or are likely to be accommodated in, the HMO.

The notice must state the maximum number of people who can occupy each room in the HMO as sleeping accommodation. Again, the landlord can appeal to an RPT.

Contravention of an overcrowding notice is a criminal offence

Management orders and overcrowding notices involve a considerable amount of local authority discretion and judgment. The above is only a very general guide, and advice should always be sought.

The Tenancy Deposit Protection Scheme

Most student landlords, particularly private landlords, ask new tenants to pay a deposit, although they are not legally obliged to do so. Although there is no legal limit on the amount of a deposit, the most common figure is one or two months' rent. The deposit that private landlords almost invariably ask for is intended to give them some financial security against any financial loss they may suffer as a result of any damage a tenant may cause to the property. It may even be termed a 'breakage deposit' or 'damage deposit' in the agreement, although these terms have no special legal significance.

Unfortunately the issue of deposits and, in particular, their non-return by landlords at the end of the agreement is a major source of dispute and friction. Some landlords seem to regard a deposit as extra rent, only to be returned reluctantly. In 2005/6 research suggested that 30 per cent of all tenants did not receive all their deposit back (the UK average rental deposit in 2005/6 was £700). A new **Tenancy Deposit Protection Scheme** (TDPS) was introduced in April 2007 along with subsequent regulations which significantly improves tenants' rights and ensures that their deposits are not unfairly withheld. Student tenants, like any other tenants, should:

* Before agreeing to pay a deposit, ask the landlord to confirm in writing exactly what the deposit covers and when the money will be returned.

* Always ask for a receipt for any deposit paid and the landlord should tell them which tenancy deposit scheme their deposit has been paid into.

* Try to ensure that the landlord gives them an inventory (a list of the contents and condition of the property) before moving in. They should check this carefully to make sure it is accurate and that everything is in working order. Then, if possible, they should agree by jointly signing the inventory with the landlord.

* If they don't receive an inventory, they should write one themselves with an independent witness, such as a friend,

and send a copy to their landlord/agent. Ask the witness to sign and date that the inventory is a true record of the condition of the property. It may even be helpful to take photographs to record the condition of the property when the students move in, perhaps even dated by (for example a suitably placed newspaper in the photograph). This record should be kept up to date during the agreement.

- Make a careful note of the state of decoration in the property, and the condition of any furniture and appliances supplied. If anything is worn, broken, or damaged they should report this in writing to their landlord and keep a copy.

- A landlord cannot withhold all, or even part, of a deposit because of general 'wear and tear'. Landlords are expected to redecorate and replace (as appropriate) carpets and furnishings every few years – perhaps even more frequently if there is a high turn over of tenants. A tenant should only be liable for damage which creates extra costs.

The new provisions

Although introduced by Part VI of the Housing Act 2004, the TDPS was only brought into effect on 6 April 2007. All deposits taken by landlords from that date are protected provided the tenancy is an **assured shorthold** one.

The new scheme only applies to **assured shorthold tenancies** (ASTs) (see Chapters 1 and 10), and not, for example, to **assured tenancies** or **licences.** The majority of student tenants occupy ASTs but this will need checking at the outset. The exception is when the student rents from their own university (eg in a traditional 'hall'). As explained in Chapter 2 such agreements (even if tenancies) are not ASTs.

When a landlord takes a deposit for an AST s/he is required to hold that deposit in accordance with one of the three designated tenancy deposit schemes (Housing Act 2004, section 213). The landlord is also required to give specific information to the tenant and to anyone who has arranged with the tenant to pay the deposit on their behalf.

If the landlord does not comply with the above requirements, s/he may not serve a **section 21 possession notice** (see Chapter 10). In such cases, tenants can apply for a court order requiring the landlord to pay them a 'fine' of three times the amount of the deposit.

The designated schemes

There are three 'approved' schemes, two of them based around insurance. The three are:

- **The Deposit Protection Service (DPS)** – the only 'custodial' deposit protection scheme. It is free to use, as it's funded entirely from the interest earned on deposits held. The service is supported by an independent dispute regulation service. Under this scheme the tenant hands their deposit to the landlord who then pays it into the scheme. At the end of the tenancy if there is no dispute between landlord and tenant, the scheme refunds the deposit as agreed (any interest left over after funding the scheme is also divided pro-rata). If there is a dispute over the return of the deposit, the scheme's alternative dispute resolution (ADR) service will be used if both parties agree, if not, the dispute will go to the county court. Any amount that is undisputed will be paid out as agreed by the parties. The scheme will continue to hold the disputed amount until the matter is legally resolved. For more information, see www.depositprotection.com

- **Tenancy Deposit Solutions Ltd (TDSL)** – an insurance-based scheme sponsored by the National Landlord Association. A fee is payable by the landlord or their agent to insure the scheme against any misappropriation of the deposit. In this scheme the landlord retains the deposit. At the end of the tenancy s/he will return it (in whole or in part) as agreed with the tenant. S/he then informs the scheme that the protection of the deposit can cease. If there is a dispute, the landlord must hand over the disputed amount to the scheme for safekeeping until the dispute is resolved. Whether or not the landlord pays the deposit, the scheme will pay the amount due to the tenant as a result of ADR (see above) or court decision within ten

days of being notified of such decision. The scheme
is then entitled to recover the money from the landlord.
See www.mydeposits.co.uk for further information.

■ **Tenancy Deposit Scheme (TDS)** – another insurance-
based deposit and ADR scheme. It builds on a scheme
established in 2003 by the Dispute Service, to provide
dispute resolution and claims handling for the lettings
industry. It operates in much the same way as TDSL,
visit www.tds.gb.com for details.

Landlords' obligations

Under Housing Act 2004, section 213, as soon as a deposit is
paid by an **assured shorthold** tenant to a landlord, the landlord
has 14 days to:

■ comply with the 'initial requirements' of the appropriate
scheme (for example TDSL requires that information
relating to the tenancy and the deposit is recorded on its
computer system)

■ give information of a prescribed kind/form to the tenant
and to anyone who has arranged with the tenant to pay
the deposit on her/his behalf.

If either of these conditions are ignored, or at any time when the
deposit is not being held in accordance with the scheme, the
landlord may not serve a **section 21 possession notice** to end
the tenancy (see Chapter 10). Therefore, in effect the Housing
Act 2004 (HA 2004) has introduced a new defence for a tenant
against possession proceedings brought under section 21. The
HA 2004, section 215 further adds that 'no section 21 notice
may be given' which means that any purported notice would be
invalid, and (even where the scheme is eventually complied with)
a new notice would have to be served.

In addition, in situations where, for any reason, the landlord is
not complying with the initial requirements of the TDPS, a tenant
can bring a county court action (or make a counter claim – see
Chapter 10) which, (if the court finds the case proven) will result
in a sum equivalent to three times the amount of the deposit
being paid to the tenant (or the person who paid the deposit on
their behalf). Whether characterised as a 'fine' or a contractual

'penalty' this is a serious deterrent for landlords trying to circumvent the scheme.

Problem cases

Three potential areas of difficulty/uncertainty suggest themselves:

* **The position of joint tenants** (see Chapters 5 and 6). Normally each tenant will pay the same deposit either individually or as a proportionate share of an overall deposit taken by the landlord. Joint tenants are collectively ('jointly and severally') liable for what happens during their joint occupation of property and any dispute is liable to be the same dispute for all of them. However, even here Communities and Local Government (CLG) suggest that 'a lead tenant should be nominated by the other tenants to deal with issues concerning the deposit'. It has to be doubted whether this will always happen, seeming to presuppose that joint tenants are a cohesive group who can readily agree. In the case of student joint tenants of a house/flat, this may well not be the case. In other cases, the deposit taken may not be the same for all tenants, or the landlord chooses to 'go into dispute' with some rather than all of the joint tenants. This could prove to be a challenge for the ADR schemes.

* **Tenancies in existence prior to 6 April 2007, but later renewed.** Generally the TDPS scheme is not retrospective, and if an assured shorthold tenancy (AST), initially taken out prior to 6 April 2007 continues after its original 'term', this will not necessarily 'trigger' the scheme concerning existing deposits. However, if, rather than simply allowing the tenant to continue in position, the landlord grants a new AST, the TDPS will probably apply, although the law could be clearer. The landlord would then have the choice of either returning the original deposit to the tenant(s) or (if s/he wishes to continue to hold it as security, in respect of the new tenancy) it must be 'protected'.

* **When is a payment a deposit?** This tricky issue is discussed in detail in Chapter 7. However, it is clear that

'rent in advance' is not a deposit, and so does not need to be 'protected'. Equally it provides no security for a landlord against tenant disrepair, or 'misbehaviour'. More difficult is the case of money taken to 'guarantee' or provide an option for the subsequent grant of a tenancy. It is suggested, in Chapter 7, that this can sometimes be seen as rent in advance. Even if not, and it is what the CLG call a 'holding deposit', it is not, per se, a deposit requiring protection. However, as the CLG points out '...if a landlord is holding a deposit in respect of a person who subsequently becomes his tenant, then the landlord must either return the holding deposit to the tenant (so that the tenant can give it to him again as a tenancy deposit) or retain it, and protect it in a scheme within 14 days of the tenant agreeing to enter into a tenancy (ie from the date that the holding deposit becomes a tenancy deposit)'.

Safety issues

There is a patchwork of statutory requirements that relate to safety issues. In parts of the country where the amount of private rented accommodation available exceeds demand, many colleges have successfully established accreditation schemes. These require landlords to provide safety certificates as a pre-requisite to letting through the college accommodation letting service. It is more difficult for colleges to impose a system like this in areas where demand exceeds supply.

Gas

Deaths and serious injuries have been caused by carbon monoxide seeping out of old or unserviced gas appliances. It is essential that the fumes from gas boilers, water heaters and fires, leave the accommodation via a chimney or piping (flue). Chimneys and flues must be kept unblocked and fully enclosed. Under the Gas Safety Regulations 1998, all landlords are responsible for ensuring that gas appliances and flues are:

- maintained in good order
- checked for safety at least every 12 months by a CORGI registered gas installer.

Landlords are obliged to keep a record of the safety checks and supply them to existing occupiers within 28 days of the check being carried out. Prospective occupiers must be given a copy of the latest check before moving in. If there are concerns about this, any tenant involved should contact their local environmental health department. Further information can also be obtained from the Gas Safety Advice Line: 0800 300 363.

Electricity

Landlords have a general responsibility for the electricity supply and the electrical appliances they provide in their accommodation. They must be able to prove that all fixed electrical installations and alterations carried out from 1 January 2005 were done and certified by a 'competent' person (Building Regulations Requirement P). In practice, many college housing services require private landlords to have certificates of electrical safety issued by the NICEIC (National Inspection Council for Electrical Installation Contracting) or ECA (Electrical Contractors Association).

Fire: safety and means of escape

All accommodation should have a clear, safe and uncluttered exit route in case of fire. In terms of the law, environmental health officers have some obligations to ensure that there are adequate means of escape from fire but only where the accommodation is regarded as a 'house in multiple occupation' (HMO – see discussion earlier in this chapter).

Given that HMOs are regarded as the least safe type of housing, landlords may be required to provide lobbies and fire-check doors and/or doors with self-closing devices along escape routes. Useful guidance on fire safety and how to carry out a fire safety risk assessment is available (see p177 for more details). Student accommodation services may require private landlords to make such provisions under their college landlord accreditation scheme (see Chapter 2).

Fire precautions

Fire precautions usually only include the provision of smoke detectors, fire extinguishers and fire blankets. There is no statutory requirement for other accommodation. However, as a bare minimum, students should acquire their own smoke detectors. The fitting of smoke detectors is often required as part of a college landlord accreditation scheme.

Furnishings and furniture

All furnishings and furniture in rented accommodation must be made of materials that have passed specified ignitability tests. This covers all kinds of seating, beds and bedding. All furniture produced since 1988 must be labelled with an indication that it complies with the Furniture and Furnishings (Fire Safety) Regulations 1988. A concerned student should contact their local Trading Standards office (TSO), as it has the power to remove unsafe items.

Insurance for landlords

All landlords should have building insurance to ensure that they have cover in the event of fire, etc, damage. It is also essential to have cover for property owners' liability and it is possible to get cover for loss of rent following damage to a building and for malicious damage caused by tenants. Some insurers regard single sharers and students as 'high risk' tenants and may decline cover or charge accordingly.

Contents insurance is necessary to cover the landlord's furnishings and fittings. Given that many tenants do not have contents insurance, cover for accidental damage caused to the landlord's contents is also frequently taken out. Employers' liability and landlords' liability insurance in relation to the contents, covers injuries to tenants or their guests caused by eg defective cookers, light fittings and loose carpets which can result in substantial compensation claims.

Emergency assistance insurance will provide help for the landlord and the tenant in the event of an emergency at the property, such as: failure of the electricity supply, failure of the cooking facilities, lost keys, plumbing problems, leaking roofs or guttering, and security of doors and windows. If there is a 24/7 helpline, the policy can be advantageous to landlord and tenant.

Rent guarantee insurance will ensure that the landlord can meet their planned outgoings. Premiums are usually calculated as percentage of the annual rent eg three to four per cent. The insurance payment should also be tax-deductible.

Landlords may also have legal expenses insurance in the event of needing to issue possession proceedings.

Insurance for tenants

Moving into rented accommodation is an expensive venture when the landlord requires a deposit and rent up front. However, tenants should ensure that they have insurance for their own possessions. Many tenants are surprised after a loss to discover that the landlord's insurance does not cover their possessions. Given that the value of students' possessions may not be high, it is worth finding a specialist tenants' insurance policy which can also cover any damage they may accidentally cause to the landlord's possessions.

Accreditation schemes

Private landlords renting to students (whether operating large 'halls', or traditional accommodation) may be part of an 'accreditation scheme'. Such schemes began on a limited basis in the early 1990s but are now widespread. They are essentially based on 'voluntary' compliance by landlords with codes of practice relating to the standards in their properties, and their relationship with their tenants. For many landlords, even though being part of a scheme is voluntary, there are likely to be practical advantages for them, eg being on some kind of approved university accommodation list.

In addition to the above, some 155 educational establishments have 'signed up' to either the Universities UK, or Accreditation Network UK's (ANUK's) codes. As a consequence they have been exempt from HMO licensing.

ANUK have also provided the model for the majority of other accreditation codes. ANUK approved schemes cover all aspects of the tenancy relationship, pre-contractual, contractual and post-contractual, and cover such matters as health and safety, misleading advertising, unfair terms, deposits, and complaints procedures. However, there are many other accreditation codes, most frequently administered by local authorities. Of these codes, 12 have been specifically designed for student housing (see www.anuk.org.uk for further information).

Fundamental do's and don'ts for landlords 4

Subjects covered in this chapter include...

Quiet enjoyment

Trespassing

Keys

Personal possessions

Harassment and unlawful eviction

Remedies

Prosecutions

All occupiers, including students, are entitled to use their accommodation without undue interference by their landlord. In most cases, the landlord is not entitled to enter the student accommodation without the student's permission. While the law does not differentiate between different types of landlord, in practice problems of this nature are most likely to arise where a private landlord is involved. Unacceptable behaviour can range from the annoying, to the extreme:

- entering the accommodation while the student is out

- trying to restrict the student's enjoyment of the accommodation

- cutting off electricity or other supplies

- harassing the student in subtle (or not so subtle) ways

- putting all the student's possessions in bin bags and changing the locks.

Such behaviour can arise where landlords see rented out accommodation as entirely their own property and thus under their exclusive control. It may be that landlords ignore the fact, or are unaware that all occupiers, including students, have contractual and legal rights. Problems can often begin when there is a dispute about rent or how the accommodation is being used. Landlords may take matters into their own hands without taking legal advice as to the correct and appropriate way forward.

Ideally low level problems are best resolved by prompt and direct communication between the landlord and the students. If this does not work, it might be helpful to bring in a third party such as the university or college accommodation service to mediate. Cases that are more serious could require the involvement of a Shelter adviser, the citizens advice bureau (CAB), a solicitor, or the local authority. Frequently (and understandably), faced with hostile behaviour and needing to restore a stable living situation, students simply leave and find new accommodation. There may well be ongoing problems for the students in recovering a deposit (see Chapters 3 and 5) but leaving does not resolve the problem for future occupiers.

Quiet enjoyment

All tenants are entitled to 'quiet enjoyment' of their accommodation through their contract with the landlord. This may be specifically included in the tenancy agreement but the law implies it in any event. Quiet enjoyment relates to the student's fundamental entitlement to use the accommodation without interference. It is difficult to define quiet enjoyment – perhaps 'undisturbed use' comes closest. Most definitions focus on lists of behaviour. The word 'quiet' does not specifically relate to noise – though quiet enjoyment can certainly cover noise.

What constitutes interference?

In serious cases that have reached the courts, the following have all been found to represent a breach of this right:

- landlord threatened the tenant through letters and by shouting and banging on the door
- landlord changed the lock and did not give the tenant a new key
- landlord cutting off mains services
- landlord spat in the tenant's face, and then broke the door lock and removed the tenant's possessions while s/he was reporting the matter to the police
- a tenant with an assured shorthold who was on holiday was locked out by the landlord
- landlord carrying out building works which caused noise and loss of privacy.

The following have been found not to be a breach:

- failure to carry out repairs (but failure to deal with the consequences of disrepair can be a breach)
- letting property with poor sound insulation (though noise that seriously interferes with a tenant's enjoyment of the property can be). In *Southwark v Mills* (1999) it was stated that 'regular and excessive' noise might constitute such a 'serious interference'.

Issues for licensees

The right to quiet enjoyment does not automatically apply
to students who are licensees, though they do have some
protection. In *Smith v Nottinghamshire County Council* (1981)
(*The Times,* 13 November) students in Sandby Hall, a hall
of residence in Nottingham, complained that it was almost
impossible to prepare for exams in their study bedrooms due to
the noise made by repair work that the university was carrying
out. The court said that the university should do nothing without
just cause to disturb the students from getting on with their
studies with 'reasonable quietude' in their rooms. This suggests
that the university could have carried out emergency work but
not disruptive repairs, which could have waited until after the
exams had finished or the end of term.

Case

A group of students approached the university accommodation
office when they found the service provided by their landlord was
in some senses too good. In response to repair requests he would
carry out repairs himself, but sit down for a cup of tea and chat
when he had finished. He would then look around the property
to find other (non-essential) repairs to carry out, and come back
shortly to carry them out and to have another chat. The students
did not like to complain as the landlord was pleasant, but he really
did outstay his welcome and interfere with their 'quiet enjoyment'.

The accommodation office contacted the landlord who was
shocked to find his visits were unwelcome. A few weeks later he
contacted the university and asked it to put the property in its
management scheme, which it agreed to do.

Comment

While this scenario may initially appear to be a minor problem, it
does highlight the basic fact that tenants are entitled to their own
space. The student rental market attracts landlords both large and
small, who sometimes do not understand their responsibilities. At
one extreme, repair requests may be ignored and, at the other,
landlords may treat the property as their own and refuse to 'let go'.

Trespassing

Landlords have no general right to enter tenants' rooms, and entering without permission constitutes trespass. It may also be a breach of the right to quiet enjoyment (see above) and harassment (see below). This is because tenants have exclusive possession of their accommodation (see Chapter 5). To overcome this problem, tenancy agreements usually contain clauses that give the landlord a right to enter. In the typical example quoted below, the landlord's rights are restricted and any entry outside its terms would be a trespass. Emergency access, for example, to fix a burst pipe while the student is away, would not be a trespass.

Example of tenancy agreement clause which allows entry by the landlord and an agent:

> *The tenant will allow the landlord at all reasonable times to enter the premises for the purpose of:*

- *repairing or painting the outside of the premises*

- *carrying out any structural or other necessary repairs to the premises*

- *examining the state and condition of the premises*

- *(in the last three months) showing the premises to prospective tenants or purchasers.*

> *In this clause, the term 'landlord' includes the landlord's agent, any superior landlord and, where necessary, trades people and others. The landlord must give reasonable prior notice of her/his intention to enter the premises during the tenancy period. In the event of an emergency, notice may not be required.*

Where the student has a genuine licence agreement, this may give the landlord a more general right to enter the student accommodation, for example, to clean the room. Such agreements would, however, only rarely be seen as genuine today, see Chapter 5.

Keys

Difficulties about keys to rooms can arise in this context.
Landlords frequently retain keys. This may be so that they can
enter the premises to provide services such as changing bed
linen, cleaning, or for access in an emergency. However,
students might want to change a lock if they are concerned
about security, for example where they suspect that the landlord
has been entering the accommodation while they were out. If
there is a common entrance shared with other occupiers of the
property, the student cannot change this lock without the
consent of the other occupiers and the landlord. As far as the
student's own room is concerned, the student does have the
right to change the lock by, for example, changing the barrel of
a Yale lock. The student's tenancy agreement may seek to forbid
this or require the student to provide a new key to the landlord.
Before following this course of action, the student should
consider possible consequences, as failing to comply with the
tenancy agreement could lead to the landlord seeking to evict
the student (see Chapter 10).

Personal possessions

In all situations, landlords should not interfere with the
student's personal possessions. To do so would also constitute
trespass. In one reported case, a landlord actually burned a
student's PhD notes (*Caruso v Owen* (1983)). Where a student
believes the landlord has taken something, s/he needs to
check with the landlord (after checking that it isn't mislaid or
a flatmate hasn't borrowed it). This could of course amount
to theft. If the student wants to take the matter further, they
will need some proof that the item actually exists and that the
landlord had access.

Harassment and unlawful eviction

Under the Protection from Eviction Act 1977, tenants and most
licensees have the legal right not to be harassed or unlawfully
evicted by their landlord. Harassment and unlawful eviction can
give rise to both a civil right to compensation from the landlord,
and criminal proceedings being taken against her/him.

Harassment is defined as:

- doing acts likely to interfere with a residential occupier's peace or comfort

- persistently withdrawing or withholding services.

One example would be the landlord refusing to allow the student to use facilities that are part of the student's letting agreement. If it was agreed that the student could use a washing machine located in a separate room, the landlord cannot unilaterally withdraw that right later. This would also apply to rights to use facilities such as a shared kitchen, bathroom, garden or shed. Cutting off the student's gas or electricity supply could constitute harassment even if there is a dispute about bills.

Unlawful eviction is committed where a landlord unlawfully deprives a residential occupier of any premises. An eviction is unlawful where a landlord has evicted an occupier without going through the correct notice and court procedures (see Chapter 10). This would be the case even if the occupier had not paid their rent or had broken the terms of the licence or tenancy agreement. One of the clearest examples would be a landlord unilaterally changing the lock on the accommodation door so that the student cannot gain access. Refusing to replace a tenant's lost key has also been held to constitute unlawful eviction.

Tenancy agreements frequently contain forfeiture clauses, which say that the landlord can 're-enter' the accommodation and end the tenancy where the occupier has broken its terms. However, landlords should be aware that in most cases the law still requires them to serve a notice on the tenant and to obtain a court possession order before evicting her/him. Without them, the eviction will be unlawful despite the forfeiture clause.

Remedies

Where a landlord's behaviour falls into any of the categories above, the student has a number of options:

- seek to get the harassment stopped

- seek compensation from the landlord for her/his bad behaviour

- recover the student's possessions

- return to the student accommodation

- have the landlord prosecuted.

Where difficulties arise, the landlord and student should keep a detailed, written record of what has happened and when. This will be useful as evidence should matters get worse. Many students worry about making complaints because they think this will lead to further problems with the landlord, but 'putting up with it' can also lead to landlords assuming that they can do what they like. The student should seek advice and support from the university or college accommodation service. A complaint can be made to the local housing authority's **Tenancy Relations Officer** (TRO). Many TROs will attempt to conciliate between landlords and tenants when disputes arise and to calm things down by talking to both parties. However, TROs have powers to make a landlord comply with the law, including taking out prosecutions (see below). See Chapter 9 for information about TROs.

Where the situation has become serious, all but the last option is likely to involve the occupier in having to instruct a solicitor to take civil proceedings against the landlord. A court action can seek all these remedies. Experienced solicitors can act very quickly to get court orders, which will order the landlord to return the student's possessions, let her/him back in, and restrain the landlord from harassing the student. A landlord who does not comply with an order can be brought before the court for contempt which could lead to a fine and/or imprisonment.

Obtaining damages (compensation) from the landlord will take longer, but it is worth bearing in mind that this kind of behaviour can be taken very seriously by the courts.

In the case of *Dimoutsikou v Penrose* (2000), a tenant who had an assured shorthold tenancy was locked out while on holiday. The court decided that the landlord had deliberately acted while the tenant was away. It ordered the landlord to pay the tenant a total of £8,438.40 damages.

The normal way of calculating damages in these cases is to compensate the tenant for losses resulting from the harassment or illegal eviction.

This could include:

- damage to, or loss of, personal belongings
- additional housing costs incurred
- legal costs.

A much higher level of damages can be awarded under section 28 of the Housing Act 1988. This is based on what the landlord has gained by evicting the tenant ie the difference between the value of the property with the tenant there, and the value of the property without the tenant.

In *Tagro v Cafane* (1991), the landlord and his agent changed the locks to the tenant's flat. The tenant had to get two injunctions to get back in, and then found his belongings gone and the flat ransacked. The court awarded £31,000 damages under section 28 plus £15,538 compensation for damage to, and loss of, possessions.

The amount of compensation available under section 28 will depend on the nature of the property. If the student is the only occupier of a property, it could be quite high. If the student is, for example, only one of a number of occupiers of bedsits in a large property, the difference between the value of the whole property with and without the student presence could be small.

If the landlord offers to re-instate the tenant before civil proceedings are begun, damages can be subsequently reduced if it was unreasonable of the tenant to refuse the offer. A reasonable refusal might involve the tenant being frightened about moving back in. Further rules say that the section 28 basis of calculation does not apply at all if the tenant is reinstated before the completion of civil proceedings. This suggests that where landlords are in the wrong, they should still offer to let the tenant back into their accommodation. However, a refusal by the tenant at this stage will not impact on their rights to compensation.

The section 28 calculation does not apply if the landlord believed (and had reasonable cause to believe) that the tenant had left the premises. It can be difficult for a landlord to decide what to do where a tenant has stopped paying rent and has left the accommodation without communicating with her/him. Caution should be exercised where some possessions have been left in the accommodation and the best advice is to obtain a possession order rather than simply empty the flat.

The amount of damages can be reduced if the tenant's conduct or that of anyone living with her/him before the eviction was 'such that it is reasonable to mitigate the damages'. The suggestion here is that in some circumstances, tenants may have brought, or partly brought the problem on themselves by breaking the terms of the tenancy agreement. This might be the case where the tenant has behaved in an antisocial way towards the landlord or other occupiers, but it may be difficult to predict the outcome where the issue is to be decided by a judge on an objective basis.

Prosecutions

In serious cases of harassment and unlawful eviction, local authorities can prosecute landlords. The maximum penalties are an unlimited fine and/or two years' imprisonment. In practice, this forms part of the work of the Tenancy Relations Officers (TROs). As noted above, many TROs see their role as conciliatory and they are reluctant to prosecute. Consequently, there are considerable variations in practice between authorities.

Generally, there are few prosecutions other than in exceptionally serious cases (see below). Some of the reasons given by authorities for their reluctance are:

- the tenant's fear of reprisals and reluctance to go to court
- difficulty with evidence (lack of corroboration and detailed records)
- the time it takes to get to court
- the high burden of proof required in criminal cases
- the cost of assembling and prosecuting the case.

However, a well-organised and well publicised case can effectively deter local landlords from indulging in this kind of illegal behaviour.

Case

Tony Carroll, a Nottingham landlord, removed the back door of a property let to Nottingham University students with a crowbar, and did not replace it for some days. There was a dispute over rent. According to the landlord, he had agreed to allow the students to live in the house over the summer, but they moved in earlier than agreed and then claimed that they owed no rent for September.

Carroll, who had 20 rented properties, was reported as saying:

'I took the door off as a way of upsetting them. The only other way to deal with these issues is to go through the courts, which can take a long time, and get the students nowhere. Normally I love renting to students'.

As a result of the landlord's actions, most of the students had to leave to live in emergency accommodation and one student was so distressed that he had to postpone his studies, returning to live with his parents.

Nottingham City Council brought a prosecution against the landlord under the Protection from Eviction Act. In March 2002, Nottingham Magistrates' Court found that Carroll had broken the law and that as a result of the incidents, the tenants had been forced to give up possession of the premises. He was fined £1,000 and ordered to pay £500 costs.

Source: *Nottingham City Council and Residential Property Investor.*

The agreement stage 5

Subjects covered in this chapter include...

Basic concepts

Tenancy agreements

Financial issues

When students find their flat or house they often feel they need to sign up immediately for fear of losing it to someone else. It should be emphasised that wherever possible, they should take a little time – not least because once a contract has been entered into, it may be difficult to walk away from without losing the deposit or risking legal action. Students should be encouraged to try to read through any agreement they are asked to sign as carefully as possible, and ideally get it checked over by someone with relevant legal knowledge and expertise. This service may be available through the college accommodation office or at the students' union.

Basic concepts

Is it a licence or a tenancy?

Not everyone paying to live in a house or flat owned by someone else has the same legal rights. The identity of the person or organisation a person rents from can have a crucial bearing on the rights they acquire. In addition, a person may be offered a contract to sign, which states that it is a **licence** rather than a **tenancy**. In such a case, caution is advised. At the very least, the fact that they have been offered something that, if legally valid, allows them significantly fewer rights, should give them cause for concern.

What is a licence?

Legally, a licence is a right to be somewhere, do something, or engage in some activity. People tend to think of the piece of paper that confers the legal right(s) as 'the licence' (as in a marriage licence or a tv licence), but what matters is the legal right(s) obtained. In relation to housing, a licence to occupy a property is a right to do so. The right is important as it stops the occupier being a trespasser, but it confers less legal status than being a tenant.

Why does this matter?

It matters because a licence confers significantly fewer legal rights than any kind of tenancy. For example:

- A **licensee** (the occupant) does not have exclusive possession (the right to internally 'manage' the property and 'exclude' others), that means that a licence agreement (if valid) can 'tie down' a person's lifestyle significantly more than a tenancy (see Chapter 4).

- A licensee has no legal security in the property and can be removed at any time by the landlord on the service of four weeks' notice, and (if necessary) the obtaining of a court order (although for 'fixed-term' licences other issues arise, see below and Chapter 10).

- A licensee does not have the automatic right to complain about the condition of the property conferred on tenants by section 11 of the Landlord and Tenant Act 1985 (see Chapter 8).

How can you tell if a person is being asked to sign a licence or a tenancy?

The first thing to do is to read the agreement. Agreements that attempt to create licences use words like **licensor** and **licensee**, rather than landlord and tenant. It is also very likely (if they have been carefully drafted) that they will deny that occupiers of the accommodation have any exclusive possession over any part of the property. It is also possible that there will be clauses which state that other (unspecified) people will have a right to share the property or even that the landlord will.

The important thing is not what the agreement says it is (although that is not completely irrelevant), but what it is intended to be in practice. In all the leading court cases on the 'lease/licence' distinction, it has been consistently stated that the court should reject 'shams' and be concerned with the 'substance and reality' of the agreement.

What this means for most students occupying property owned by a private landlord, is that even an agreement which claims to be a licence is likely to be viewed as a tenancy. In most cases it will be very unlikely that the landlord intends to share with the student(s) or impose other occupiers on them against their will. The reality is that they will have exclusive possession in practice.

The main exceptions are:

* Where the property owner provides meals and/or cleaning or other services, the occupant is, in effect, a lodger in their property.

* Where the person lives in a house or flat with other occupiers who are not joint tenants with them (see below) and tends to move around the property as people come and go to the extent that no room can be said to be exclusive.

(The second situation is legally difficult and further legal advice should be taken.)

For the key cases on the above see *Street v Mountford* (1985) and *AG Securities v Vaughan/Antoniades v Villiers* (1990). *Street* is the classic example of a landlord trying to claim that a tenant was a licensee merely because her agreement said so, even though she had exclusive possession of her bedsit. The court held that a tenancy existed in practice despite the wording of the agreement. The case of *Antoniades* further illustrates that flat-sharers who signed apparently independent licence agreements were actually joint tenants. Their agreements were interdependent because in reality they occupied the flat jointly to the exclusion of anyone else. In *Vaughan*, the four flat-sharers only had individual licences, principally because they moved around to the extent that no room could be said to be exclusively theirs.

Is the position any different for other 'landlords'?

This is a difficult question. If the 'reality' of a university running a hall of residence or a council running a hostel is considered, it should be fairly clear that licences are more likely to exist simply because the exceptions mentioned above are more likely to arise. It is common for people to have to move round a hostel at short notice as others move in. It is not uncommon for universities to provide lodger/'hotel' type services in halls of residence.

However, it may be that the 'rules' are a little different as well. In *Westminster City Council v Clarke* (1992) the occupant of a council hostel for vulnerable homeless single men was said to be a licensee, not a tenant. This was partly because the occupants of the hostel did not have exclusive possession (partly because of the supervisory presence of council staff, partly because of a clause in his agreement indicating he might have to be moved around the hostel as circumstances required). However, another factor was the difficulties the council would face in managing such a hostel if the occupants were tenants.

What significance might this have for students? It would be unusual for students, even if occupants of council or registered social landlord properties, to be in hostels. *Clarke* does not suggest that council or registered social landlords (RSLs) have an absolute dispensation to create licences where private landlords do not. Perhaps the issue is most interesting in relation to halls of residence.

Universities might argue that traditional catered and closely supervised halls are a natural place for licences to exist. This seems broadly correct.

Even in other halls where no services are provided and there is little close supervision, the university is in a distinct position. On the analogy of *Clarke*, its responsibilities to the wider community (or at least the wider student community) and the difficulties it might face if it could not 'discipline' students by moving them or removing them, should lead the courts to be more sympathetic to claims of licences. This is, however, much more uncertain (see Chapter 2).

Oral agreements – are they binding?

In general, yes. The law does not usually require tenancy or licence agreements to be in writing (there are exceptions regarding some types of long-term tenancies, particularly fixed-term leases for three years or more, but they are very unlikely to affect students). However, establishing the legal consequences of an oral agreement is more difficult. Suggestions are given below.

It is not uncommon for a student to move into a property without having signed a written contract. It may be in such cases that a contract has been given to the occupier but they don't sign before moving in. In some cases, however, no written contract exists at all. In these circumstances what is known as an 'oral agreement' applies.

The oral agreement is more likely to be a tenancy than a licence. Except in the self-evident cases like hotels and hostels, licences need to be specifically created and the 'fall back' position is a tenancy.

What type of tenancy it is depends largely on who the landlord is. In the case of private landlords, since 28 February 1997 any tenancy, written or oral, is an **assured shorthold** unless the landlord states otherwise.

In the highly unlikely situation that the student went into possession of the property before 28 February 1997 (the date when the relevant parts of the Housing Act 1996 came into force) they might find that they have better legal rights. This is because most written agreements would have been offered as **assured shorthold tenancies** (see Chapter 10), whereas their status under the oral agreement would be as an **assured tenant**.

The tenancy will be a **periodic** rather than a **fixed-term** one (see below) because fixed-term tenancies need to be specifically created. The type of periodic tenancy will depend upon the manner in which rent is paid – if paid weekly, it will be a weekly tenancy, if paid monthly, a monthly tenancy and so on.

The issue of whether the student is a sole or joint tenant depends on questions such as whether they approached the landlord or their agent as a group, and how rent is paid (see below).

Working out the 'terms' of an oral tenancy is difficult. You might think there are no 'terms' because nothing is in writing. However, a contractual term can be 'implied' as well as 'expressed', so that an apparently blank oral agreement can be filled out with terms to a degree. Some terms are implied by statute, for example the term as to landlords' repairing obligations contained in section 11 of the Landlord and Tenant Act 1985 (see Chapter 8). If there is a written agreement but the student didn't sign it before moving in, it may be that terms from the written agreement will be implied in the oral agreement. (This is not certain and if it is important, legal advice should be sought.)

Other terms are implied as a result of what is a normal expectation of an agreement of that type (see for example the obligation of a tenant to act in a 'tenant-like' manner, also discussed in Chapter 8).

Whether it is wise for a student to move in without a signed contract is more doubtful. The legal position is definitely less clear, particularly when considering the detailed terms under which a person occupies. Also, it has to be asked why a written agreement was not produced by the landlord – it may suggest that there is something to worry about, for example, that they have a mortgage on the property that prohibits tenancies?

In a few cases it may not be clear whether the agreement is in writing or not. Perhaps the two commonest situations are:

- agreements made electronically
- written agreements which are never signed.

As regards electronic agreements (which are becoming increasingly common in relation to landlords who let on a large scale to students) the best analysis is probably information on a website (or similar) about available accommodation. If the student makes an application for particular accommodation advertised this way, they are offering to live there on the basis of the terms and other details laid out on the website. Once the landlord accepts the application, there is a contract based on these written details.

If, subsequently, the student is sent a tenancy agreement to sign and return, they should check it first. If they find the written agreement contains additional information or obligations they are not happy with, they should take advice before signing and returning. It may be that they are not legally bound by these extra provisions.

As regards written agreements which are never signed, the best analysis is probably that the student has agreed to the written terms in the agreement given to them by their conduct in moving into the property, and continuing to live there without objecting to the terms and/or proposing alternatives.

Periodic and fixed-term tenancies

A **periodic tenancy** in law is one that needs to be continually renewed. So a weekly or a monthly tenancy needs to be renewed every week or monthly. However, there is no need to do this formally as every time the rent is paid and/or the student remains in the property, this is viewed as 'renewing' the tenancy.

A **fixed-term tenancy** is one that is 'fixed' for a specified period of time, for example an academic term, six months or the academic year.

What are the main differences between periodic and fixed-term tenancies?

A person can end a periodic tenancy by serving a valid **notice to quit** on their landlord. This has to be a minimum four weeks' notice even if it is a weekly tenancy. A landlord's position concerning termination of periodic tenancies depends on the type of tenancy involved (see Chapter 10). A fixed-term tenancy cannot be brought to an end before the expiry of its normal term by the service of a notice to quit, but only by the exercise of a 'break clause' in the agreement (if there is one).

A tenant is normally bound by a fixed term-tenancy for the period specified in the agreement. This means s/he will generally not be able to leave before the end of this period. Most tenancies or licences that are encountered today are likely to be fixed-term ones, since landlords see fixed-term agreements as providing them with greater financial security (in that the rent of the property is guaranteed for the period specified). It is unlikely that there will be a 'get out' ('break') clause in the agreement allowing the tenant to leave (although fixed-term hall of residence agreements often make exceptions covering illness or other emergencies). Many students wrongly believe that they have a right to leave accommodation they occupy under a fixed-term agreement for personal reasons, most typically because they do not get on with other residents. This is not true – the circumstances in which they can leave (assuming there is no 'break' clause in the agreement) are very limited, being largely confined to the unfitness of the property (see Chapter 8).

If a student does enter into a fixed-term agreement and later regrets it, it may be possible for them to negotiate matters with their landlord. The landlord may be willing to compromise, even though in strict law they can look to the student for their rent until a substitute acceptable to them is found (by the student or landlord). (For more information on rent, see Chapter 7.)

Joint and sole tenancies

A **joint tenancy** occurs wherever more than one person in a property shares a tenancy. In legal parlance joint tenants do not possess separate parts of the property, they are all equally entitled to joint exclusive possession of the whole of it. Joint tenants collectively possess one tenancy.

A **sole tenant**, even if they live under the same roof as others, only has a right to exclusive possession of any accommodation they separately occupy (typically their bedroom) although there may be joint use of other rooms such as kitchens and bathrooms.

How do you distinguish between a 'joint' and a 'sole' tenancy?

This is a difficult question. As always there are obvious cases; at one extreme the 'bedsit' occupier, even if a tenant, is obviously a sole tenant. At the other extreme, a group of friends approach a landlord's agent together, and sign one tenancy agreement containing all their names, following which they continue to occupy the property together and pay one rent for the whole. This is clearly a joint tenancy. However, other cases will be more uncertain, particularly where a number of occupiers live under the same roof and share some expenses, but pay separate rents to their landlord (not uncommon in student tenancies). An already complicated question is often made even more difficult by the confusion with the linked but distinct question as to whether the occupiers share a 'single household' and so do not occupy a 'house in multiple occupation' (see Chapter 3).

There is no single or simple test to decide whether a tenancy is sole or joint, but pointers include:

* whether the tenancy contract is in joint names or (alternatively) there are several individual contracts

* how the rent is paid, jointly or individually, and whether the property is stated to be let for one overall rent or a number of individual rents

* whether the tenants first approached the landlord or their agent as a couple/group or separately

* whether the tenants share – in any sense – a 'single household'. Although this is not crucial in isolation, as stated above, it may be a relevant factor in some cases. A 'single household' is one where the occupiers look after the property together and share expenses.

Why is the distinction important?

The distinction is important because sole tenants are only liable for their own rent and have only very limited liability for what other tenants do. Conversely, joint tenants are jointly responsible so that rent is owed collectively and there is equivalent liability for breakages and disrepair. So, if a joint tenant 'walks away' from a fixed-term tenancy, instead of regarding them as responsible for unpaid rent, the landlord can look to the remaining joint tenants to make up the difference. If an agreement, tenancy or licence, seeks to make sole occupiers jointly liable for matters like breakages this is, arguably, an unfair contract term and unenforceable (see later in the chapter).

Being a joint tenant confers joint rights over the whole property occupied. A joint tenancy is one entire tenancy, not a number of interlinked ones. So if, for example, one joint tenant leaves, although the others remain liable for their rent, they probably have the right to allow others into the property as their 'guests' (licensees) to, perhaps, help offset the cost.

Case

Four female students shared a house as joint tenants. One of the group, Rachel, sought advice when she wished to leave to live with her boyfriend. She had found a replacement male student but the others had objected and she felt they were being unreasonable and unnecessarily spiteful. She was advised about joint liability, but that the group as a whole had to be realistic. She was further advised to try and persuade the others to accept her nominated replacement if there was no valid reason to reject him, which there did not seem to be: he was in the same year at the same university, had a genuine reason for needing accommodation mid-year, and was willing to pay the final term's rent immediately. However, the others still refused to accept him, and they did nothing to advertise the potentially vacant room or show it to prospective tenants.

Rachel came back to the accommodation office as relations within the house were strained. The joint liability was again emphasised, but she was advised that if she did decide to move out she would explain the whole situation to the landlord and inform him with whom she had left her key – or hand it to him. She moved out, and the landlord threatened to take the remaining students to court for the unpaid balance of Rachel's rent, which they eventually paid between them.

Comment

The landlord could have held all the tenants liable for the rent, including Rachel, but in a situation like this, it is important to keep the landlord informed. The landlord may choosen to ask any one of them for the unpaid rent. Similarly, a tenant who has simply not paid while living in the property may be sued for her/his share of the rent, but the others in the group are equally liable in law for the debt.

Tenants under 18

If a student is under 18 when they make an agreement to rent accommodation, the law is rather different – and not particularly satisfactory. A person under 18 can enter into a valid contract because even though they are under age, the law regards contracts for necessities like food and shelter as ones you can legally enter into. However, a person under 18 cannot hold what is termed a 'legal estate' and given that a tenancy is a form of legal estate, a person under 18 cannot hold a tenancy.

However:

- recent case law suggests that an attempt to create a tenancy with someone under 18 results in a contract to 'convey' the 'legal estate' once they reach 18

- a licence is not a 'legal estate' and so a person under 18 can validly hold a licence to occupy property

- another approach which councils have used is to grant a tenancy to another person (such as a social worker) to hold on behalf of the under 18 year old until they reach 18.

Although most students are 18 when they begin their studies, and so enter into accommodation agreements, it is not so uncommon for a first year to be under 18. It is highly unsatisfactory that the law in this area if 'fuzzy'. In any case of doubt or uncertainty, expert legal advice should be sought.

Tenancy agreements

Is a student legally bound by all terms in an agreement they have signed?

It is wise to assume that the answer is 'yes'. As a general principle, a person is bound by what they sign even if they have failed to read the agreement. However:

- Some terms may be 'unfair' and so unenforceable in relation to the Unfair Terms in Consumer Contracts Regulations 1999. These regulations also apply to licences and tenancies. (The regulations are discussed further below.)

- Some terms may be invalid in law. For example, if a landlord seeks to transfer responsibility for keeping a property in repair (see Chapter 8) to her/his tenants, this has no legal effect (you cannot 'contract out' your basic legal rights).

- Some terms may be inconsistent with other occupiers' rights guaranteed by law. For example, if a tenancy agreement attempts to give a landlord unrestricted access to the property at all times, this seems to be inconsistent with the tenants' right to 'quiet enjoyment' (see Chapter 4). A term which prohibits an occupant from having guests staying with them in the property seems to be inconsistent with a tenant's (although not a licensee's) right of exclusive possession.

- Some terms may be unenforceable because their effect has been misrepresented earlier by the landlord or the landlord's agent.

Can a tenant cancel an agreement they have entered into?

Generally, the answer is no. A tenant is bound by agreements they have signed or otherwise entered into unless they have been the victim of fraud, misrepresentation or undue influence (the latter are matters of general contract law which are beyond the scope of this book).

However, if someone enters into the agreement electronically, over the telephone, or via some other form of 'distance communication' (see below) the situation might be different. It may be that in such cases the Consumer Protection (Distance Selling) Regulations 2000 apply – and there is a right to cancel the agreement within seven days of entering into it.

The principal 'distance communication' circumstances listed in the regulations (Schedule 1) are:

- mail order
- letter
- telephone
- radio
- electronic mail
- fax.

The Distance Selling Regulations are not entirely clear as to which contracts they apply to, and conflicting views have been expressed as to whether they apply to tenancy agreements. However, the Office of Fair Trading (OFT) seems to think that they do apply. If it seems that the Regulations may apply, and if the student is within the seven day cancellation period, they should take legal advice immediately.

Unfair contract terms

Traditionally contract law was governed by the principle of 'freedom of contract'. In essence, if a student agrees to something s/he is bound by it – no matter how 'unfair' or one-sided. Exceptions to this principle were limited to arguing that the term in question was unclear/ambiguous and any doubt should be resolved in favour of the 'victim' (the so-called 'contra proferentem' principle) or that no real agreement had taken place. In the latter case, this exception largely applied to oral contracts where it could sometimes be argued that insufficient 'notice' had been given of the term in question before the agreement had been entered into. In the case of written and signed contracts (which most tenancy agreements are), a person is usually 'bound' by their signature unless the term in question is in such small print as to be illegible or they were the victim of fraud or misrepresentation.

All the above exceptions still hold good, but increasingly 'freedom of contract' has been curbed by legislation seeking to achieve a fairer balance in contractual rights and duties. Of particular general significance are the Unfair Contract Terms Act 1977, and the Unfair Terms in Consumer Contract regulations (first enacted in 1995 but now in a 1999 version). The Unfair Contract Terms Act does not apply to tenancy agreements per se (although it may have relevance to allied areas – see Chapter 2). Initially it was a matter of some debate as to whether the Unfair Terms in Consumer Contracts Regulations (UTCCR) applied to tenancy agreements – however, it is now clear that they do (see *R C Khatun and others v Newham London Borough Council* (2005)). Indeed the OFT see tenancy agreements as an area of particular importance in curbing unfairness in consumer contracts. On 7 September 2005 the OFT issued detailed guidance on Unfair Terms in Tenancy Agreements (OFT 356).

This guidance can be downloaded from the OFT website (www.oft.gov.uk). The area of tenancy agreements is of prime concern to the OFT as they receive more than 200 complaints every year about unfair terms in standard tenancy contracts, such as financial penalties, exclusions of the landlord's liability for repairs, and unfair termination and eviction clauses. Between 1996 and 2006, 70 tenancy agreements, which had been referred to the OFT, had been declared incompatible with the UTCCR and had had some of their terms replaced, or been totally replaced with new agreements approved by the OFT. Seventeen of these references were made specifically in respect of student tenancies, and some 310 terms were either deleted or modified as a result.

The structure of the UTCCR could be clearer, but in outline (see UTCCR regulation 5 in particular):

i)   they apply to terms which have not been 'negotiated' (it seems doubtful if most students negotiate with their landlords over the details of their tenancy agreements)

ii) once they do apply, any term is 'unfair' if they are:

- 'contrary to requirement of good faith'

- a 'significant imbalance in the parties rights'

- 'to the detriment of the consumer'.

Taking all this together it suggests that a term should be seen as unfair if it is 'one-sided' and that this 'one-sidedness' results from an unequal relationship. Again it seems fairly clear that this can be said of most landlord and tenant relationships. In addition, regulation 7 requires that tenancy agreements be 'laid out' in 'plain and intelligible' language.

When trying to decide whether a particular clause in a particular tenancy agreement is unfair, refer the agreement to the OFT for their view. A 'feel' for what the OFT view is likely to be, can be gleaned from looking at the guidance mentioned above, and from examples of terms found to be unfair by the OFT which are outlined in their regular 'bulletins', also available on the OFT website. In addition, Schedule 2 of the UTCCR contains a (so called) 'indicative and non-exhaustive' list of terms that may be unfair – examples include disclaimers of liability, one-sided cancellation clauses, clauses allowing unilateral variation of contract terms, and 'disproportionate' fixed penalty clauses.

Typical examples of terms modified or deleted by the OFT include:

* Terms binding tenants to documents they may not have had a copy of prior to signing the tenancy agreements.

* Terms giving landlords unrestricted access to the property.

* Terms with the potential for transferring landlords' obligations to the tenant, for example in relation to repairs (see Chapter 8).

* Terms withholding vital information, such as that the landlord is required to obtain a court order before a tenant can be evicted.

* Terms making a person liable for all damage and undue wear and tear in 'collectively' occupied accommodation (for example a hall of residence) regardless of their fault in causing the damage.

In addition, the OFT has frequently invoked regulation 7 (above) to require the deletion of legal jargon and to require a clearer layout. Expressions that have been deleted include 'joint and several liability', 'indemnify', 'vitiate' and 'liquidated damages'.

Theoretically, the OFT need not be involved and an individual tenant can challenge a particular tenancy term as unfair in the county court. In practice, it is not normally to be recommended.

Guarantors

It is becoming increasingly common for landlords to want parents or someone similar to 'underwrite' student rent. If a student is under 18 (see above), this is almost always the case. In legal terms, if a person contracts to occupy property as a tenant or licensee, they are the major potential debtor and their landlord can always look to them for unpaid rent. However, if they are unable, or unwilling to pay, they may seek to enforce the debt against any person who has 'guaranteed' it.

Rent undertaking – liability of guarantors

A guarantor is only liable to pay if the main debtor is also liable. So, if for any reason the main tenancy or licence contract is unenforceable, the guarantee is unenforceable as well. A guarantee is only enforceable if it is either in writing or where there is some written evidence of it, and it has been signed by the guarantor or their agent.

A guarantee may on closer examination not be a guarantee at all, but rather what is termed an 'indemnity'. This is important because in theory a verbal indemnity is enforceable.

What is the difference between a rent undertaking guarantee and an indemnity?

The simple, but rather unhelpful, answer is that it depends on what the parties intend. In practice, it will depend on the words used. If the agreement seems to underwrite the debt come what may, it is an indemnity, while if it merely promises to pay if the main debtor is liable to pay, and fails to do so, it is a guarantee.

However, in general a tenant will usually be liable for any rent commitment they have given, so that a rent guarantor will be liable whether they have technically made a guarantee or an indemnity.

Also note that if a parent or other rent guarantor does have to underwrite a student's rent, they can in theory pursue them later for what they have had to pay out.

Financial issues

Deposits

Most of the important points relating to deposits and the **Tenancy Deposit Protection Scheme** (TDPS) are discussed in Chapter 3. However, it should be noted that not all money changing hands prior to a tenant entering a property are necessarily deposits covered by TDPS – they may be premiums, or agency charges, advance rent, or even retainers. In addition, prior to the introduction of the TDPS on 6 April 2007, the OFT had viewed as unfair terms whereby a landlord could retain an entire deposit if a student withdrew from a course, or was asked to leave by a university (and so wished to withdraw from the tenancy agreement) – see OFT bulletins 8, 15 and 27/28.

Premiums

In the highly unlikely event that a student has a Statutory Rent Act tenancy, it is illegal for them to be charged a fee (often called a premium) simply for the privilege of being granted the tenancy (see section 119 of the Rent Act 1977). However, premiums can be validly charged in relation to other tenancies or licence agreements. The practice is not very common in relation to student tenancies and licences. If a student is asked to pay a premium (which is non-returnable at the end of the agreement) it might cause them to think twice about entering into the agreement, particularly if the sum involved is substantial. Also, they should be careful to check whether they are being asked to pay a premium, or simply rent in advance (or both). Paying rent in advance simply means that no rent should be owing from them at the end of the tenancy (although it may weaken their tactical position concerning disrepair if they pay rent in advance – see Chapter 8 and if they do qualify for housing benefit, this is paid in arrears – Chapter 7).

Accommodation agency charges

It is illegal for an accommodation agency to charge someone a fee simply for putting them on an agency's books, or supplying them with a list of possible accommodation.

Retainers

Whereas it is relatively uncommon for students to be asked to pay a premium, it is relatively common for them to be asked to pay a retainer or holding deposit. The reason for this is that students commonly look for properties in the period from March to June, while only tending to move in from September. There is nothing unlawful about being asked to pay a retainer, but unfortunately, the legal implications of doing so are far from clear.

One interpretation is that the retainer is simply a charge for the eventual 'grant' of the tenancy (in other words it is, effectively, a premium, and so non-refundable). This may be plausible in some cases but seems an unlikely interpretation if the retainer is expressed as a weekly charge covering the period between signing the agreement and moving in.

Another interpretation is that the retainer is a payment for a guarantee that a person will be granted the tenancy (ie a kind of 'option' over it). In such a case, the retainer would only be refundable if the student goes ahead. Again, if the 'retainer' is expressed as a weekly charge covering the period after signature, it cannot be seen as merely the acquiring of an option, if for no other reason than that both parties are legally bound by the contract once it is signed.

Finally, a payment described as a retainer or holding deposit may, in fact, be rent covering the initial period of the tenancy. It is not uncommon to find a clause that half the rent needs to be paid from the period the agreement is signed, until some later date (typically near the start of the next academic year) when the full rent 'kicks in'. This could be viewed as the creation of a tenancy, with all its attendant rights and duties on both sides, from the date of signature. If so, the student would be entitled to use the property, and claim exclusive possession over it from this date. In our experience the issue is not merely academic, particularly as it is not unknown for landlords to fill up the property with another short-term occupant prior to the date when full rent becomes payable. If a tenancy does exist, the landlord who did this would be in breach of the covenant of quiet enjoyment (see Chapter 4).

There seems to be no case law on this issue and it is open to debate. A student should clarify with their landlord what rights they intend them to acquire by paying the retainer, and get their response in writing. If they are not happy with the response, it is probably safer not to go ahead, and if a dispute arises later, to take legal advice.

Sharing accommodation 6

Subjects covered in this chapter include...

Sharing issues

Sharing with family/family friend

Flat sharing arrangements

Organising the payment of bills

Sharing issues

Where a student lives in the same property as her/his landlord, this can impact on the fundamental rights and obligations that exist between the landlord and student. Where one student is the main tenant of a property and other students share with them, the main tenant takes the role of landlord to the others and the same basic rules apply. The law differentiates between two different degrees of sharing with a landlord:

The student has a room in the same house as the landlord or a self-contained flat within the landlord's house

Where a landlord is occupying the property as their only or principal home, it is not possible for the student to be either an **assured** or **assured shorthold tenant**. Instead, they are likely to be categorised as being a **non-assured occupier**. This means that the landlord can ask the student to leave by giving them a minimum of four weeks' notice in writing. No particular reasons are required for asking the student to leave. After the expiry of the notice, where the student does not leave, the landlord must obtain a court possession order against the student. However, it should be noted that a landlord is not regarded as living in the same property as the student where the property is a purpose-built block of self-contained flats.

The student shares some accommodation with the landlord or a member of the landlord's family

Virtually any degree of sharing will lead to the student being categorised as an **excluded occupier**. The only sharing that is ignored for these purposes is the shared use of a storage area or a staircase, passage, corridor or other means of access that is used by both the landlord and the student. The sharing can be with the landlord or a member of the landlord's family provided this is their only, or principal home. It is thus not possible for a landlord to keep some personal possessions in one room in a number of rented out properties and claim to be resident in them all.

Excluded occupiers are entitled to a notice period where they have an agreement that specifies one, but it is not uncommon in these situations merely to have an oral agreement. The student will only be entitled to a notice period equivalent to the rental period (eg a week or month). If the student is a tenant, the notice period can only expire at the end of a complete rental period. If s/he does not leave at that point, the landlord could evict without a court possession order though advice should be sought to ensure no possible criminal offences are committed.

Sharing with family/family friend

In some circumstances when living away from home, it may be convenient for a student to stay with another member of their family or a family friend. When this works well, it can provide a supportive living environment but in terms of rights, the student's status in the accommodation is likely to be fragile.

Where the arrangement is not regarded as being made on a commercial basis, the student is likely to be classed as a licensee rather than a tenant. A commercial letting will include some element of exclusive possession on the part of the student and the payment of a market rent. However, where there is no or a low rent, the provision by the student of some services for the landlord could constitute a rental payment. These could include cleaning or personal services. (See Chapter 5 for more details about exclusive possession and licences.) The provision of meals and/or cleaning services by the landlord is also a very strong indication of a licence.

In any event, where the landlord lives in the same property, the student will at best be a **non-assured occupier**. Where there is sharing of some of the accommodation with the landlord, the student may be an excluded occupier and have even less housing rights (see Chapter 10).

Flat sharing arrangements

Most students will either not be able to afford to rent on their own, or will want to share with other students. The ways in which the tenancy is organised can have serious implications for everyone involved. Some thought needs to be given to this before the agreement is signed. When a tenancy is being granted, the landlord may only be prepared to have all the students signed up as tenants. However, the situation may be different where a student moves in with existing tenants and there is already an existing tenancy agreement. The various possible scenarios are considered below.

Each student signs the tenancy as a joint tenant with the others

The law restricts the number of people who can be named as joint tenants in the tenancy agreement to **four**. If there are more than four, only the first four will be the **legal joint tenants**. Anyone else will be regarded as an **equitable tenant**. The legal tenants will have all the rights and responsibilities of the tenancy though they should consult with the equitable tenants before making major decisions about the tenancy.

Each legal tenant is regarded as being 'jointly and severally' liable for all aspects of the tenancy. This means each could be held individually responsible by the landlord for the payment of all the rent.

Where the tenancy is for a fixed period of time, it cannot usually be brought to an end by the joint tenants before that period expires. However, if the tenancy is periodic ie has no fixed end date and simply runs on a weekly or monthly basis, any one of the joint tenants can bring the whole tenancy to an end by giving notice to the landlord. This is an area on which a student needs o take legal advice before taking action as there has been a recent court decision which says that this may infringe the human rights of the other tenants (*McCann v UK* (ECHR 13/05/08, application 19009/04)).

One student signs as the sole tenant; the other students are sub-tenants of the sole tenant

Where one student takes on a tenancy on their own, they will be solely responsible for the rent as the main tenant. The nature of any other student occupiers' housing rights can vary depending on the particular arrangements. The other students will be regarded as sub-tenants if they have rented a self-contained part of the accommodation from the main tenant and do not share any part of the accommodation with them. If they have no self-contained accommodation, they are likely to be licensees of the main tenant (see below).

Given that this is a sharing arrangement, the main tenant will be living in the same property as the sub-tenants. This means that the sub-tenants will be at best **non-assured tenants** of the main tenant. Where there is sharing of some of the accommodation with the main tenant, the sub-tenant may be an **excluded occupier** and have few housing rights (see Chapter 10).

The law does not allow assured and assured shorthold tenants to sub-let without the landlord's permission. If there has been no permission and the main tenant gave up the tenancy, the sub-tenants would have to leave. If the sub-tenants are there with the permission of the landlord and the main tenant left, it is possible for the sub-tenants to acquire the same status that the departing tenant had. If, for example, the departing tenant was an assured shorthold tenant, the sub-tenants could become direct assured shorthold tenants of the landlord. Where a landlord knows of a sub-letting and continues to accept rent, this may amount to an implied granting of permission.

One student signs as the sole tenant; the other students are licensees of the main student tenant

The main student tenant is again solely responsible to the landlord for the rent. The other student occupiers will be regarded as licensees of the main tenant if the flat operates as a genuine flat share. This would be the situation where the other students share any part of the accommodation with the main tenant and don't have any self-contained accommodation. The other student occupiers are in a fairly weak position in terms of housing rights. They can be asked to leave by the main tenant by being given some notice that their licence arrangements will be ending (see above). For these purposes, the main tenant is in the role of a resident landlord to the other students (see Chapter 10).

Organising the payment of bills

There are two different approaches to organising the payment of utility bills such as gas, electricity, water rates, internet access and telephone:

- the sharers can all put their names down as account holders for each supplier

* different sharers can sign up individually to different utility accounts.

When moving in, the students should notify the utility suppliers. An application form indicating that they want a supply is usually required though in most cases this can be done over the phone. The sharers can list the names of all the people who will be living in the property and get each one to sign the form. Each person is then liable on a 'joint and several' basis. This means any one person can be held responsible for the whole bill.

Where only one person is named on an account, the utility company will only seek payment from them. The named person will pay the bill and then recover contributions from the other sharers. Splitting responsibility for accounts between different sharers can provide the basis of shared responsibility. It would be a good idea for the sharers to make an agreement between themselves spelling out each person's liability for the payment of bills in the event of dispute.

Some sharers set up a joint 'household' bank account with each person making regular contributions to the account. This can obviously help spread the costs and ensure that nobody is left owing very large sums. Bills can be paid via standing orders or direct debit payments to the utility companies.

Rent and other payments

7

Subjects covered in this chapter include...

What is rent?

Providing rent books

Increasing the rent payable

Challenging the rent

The obligation to pay rent

Council tax

Council tax benefit

Housing benefit

Whether a person lives in a hall of residence, rents from a private landlord, or has any kind of 'social' tenancy, one thing is constant – they have to pay to live there. What they pay may be as described as rent or as a licence charge or fee. The amount they agree to pay at the outset may be increased while they are living there, or (in a few cases) they may be able to get it reduced. They may be asked to pay a premium before they are allowed to move in. (A premium is, effectively, a charge made for allocating the property to them, see Chapter 5.) They will normally be asked to pay some kind of deposit before they move in (which they should get in full when they leave – see Chapters 3 and 5).

If the student leaves the property before the law allows them to, or without giving any notice, they will normally be liable to their landlord for any outstanding rent or licence charges. If they are a joint tenant, they will normally be liable for any unpaid rent on the property jointly occupied and not just for their own share of the rent. If the whole property they live in is occupied by other students, or if they live in a hall of residence, there should be no liability to council tax concerning the property. If they are liable, in a few cases they may be eligible for council tax benefit (CTB). In situations similar to those where council tax benefit is payable they may be eligible for housing benefit (HB) to help with the rent. Unfortunately most students do not qualify.

What is rent?

Rent is the payment that a tenant is bound by contract to make to their landlord for the exclusive possession of the property let. In almost all student tenancies, there will be a rent to be paid, and it will be expressed in money terms (although strictly a tenancy can exist without a rent being payable).

Before moving in, students should check the following (ideally their landlord or letting agent should confirm in writing):

- How much rent is payable and what it includes – for example, if it includes any other bills such as gas, electricity, water, telephone or council tax (although in the case of student tenancies it should not normally include council tax).

- When rent/bills are due – rent is usually paid weekly, monthly, or termly in advance, with the first payment due when they move in.

- How they should pay – they may be asked to pay by cheque, cash, credit card, standing order, or direct debit. If they pay cash, they should be advised to always make sure that they are given a receipt. Their landlord may ask for post-dated cheques in advance to cover future rent. This is particularly likely where rent is paid termly. Although banks disapprove of this practice, it is legal. A student tenant must decide how comfortable they feel about this (and not forgetting that a fee will be payable to their bank if they subsequently cancel a cheque).

- Whether there are any clauses in the tenancy agreement that allow the rent to be increased (see below).

The following are not rent:

- premiums for the grant of the tenancy (see Chapter 5)

- service or utility charges (such as gas, water, electricity or telephone bills)

- council tax (although a student is generally not liable to pay this)

- licence charges/payments

- payments made to a landlord after a tenancy has come to an end and before (any) renewals – these are normally referred to as mesne profits

- 'damage' deposits (see Chapters 3 and 5). These may be expressed as a multiple of the rent. They should not be confused with payments of rent in advance, which some landlords also demand.

On a practical level, it is important to distinguish premiums, deposits and service charges from rent. Also, deposits for breakage, premiums and service/utility charges are not 'eligible rent' for housing benefit purposes in those cases where students can claim housing benefit. If a student becomes potentially vulnerable to eviction for non-payment of rent (see Chapter 10), it is important to check whether any or all of the debt due relates to rent. It is not particularly significant which payments to a landlord are rent, or which are licence fees, or 'mesne profits'. All of these are 'eligible rent' for housing benefit purposes (although whether something is rent or 'mesne profits' can be very important as regards implying a new tenancy by acceptance of rent).

Providing rent books

If a tenant pays rent weekly they must have a rent book unless the rent includes a substantial proportion for food and other services. If they have to have a rent book, it should include:

- the name and address of their landlord and of the landlord's agent, if they have one

- the rent payable

- information about rights to protection from eviction

- information about agencies which can give further advice.

If the landlord fails to supply an appropriate rent book when it is a legal requirement, they are guilty of a criminal offence.

Of course, a rent book is, above all, evidence of the rent paid. If there is one, the student should make sure it is kept up to date by their landlord. If there isn't one, but there should be one by law, the student must make sure they get one. If they don't have one, and there is no legal obligation on their landlord to provide one, they should always try to get something in writing from the landlord or their agent acknowledging that they have paid (eg a receipt).

If a rent book is not required (most students pay their rent monthly or termly so there is no legal requirement to provide one), the amount of rent and method of payment should be clearly indicated in the tenancy (or licence) agreement. This assumes that there is a written agreement. If there isn't, the student should ask the landlord about this and ask for something in writing.

If the student has an **assured shorthold tenancy** (see Chapters 1 and 10) which began on, or after, 28 February 1997 and they have no written agreement, or the agreement does not contain details of rent, they have a right to request a written statement of the following:

- the amount of rent payable and when it should be paid
- any arrangements for increasing the rent
- the date the tenancy began and the length of any fixed term.

It is illegal for a landlord not to provide a tenant with such astatement within 28 days of receiving a request in writing (section 20A of the Housing Act 1988, as amended).

Increasing the rent payable

The first thing to do is to check whether a tenancy (or licence) agreement specifies any procedure for rent to be increased. Unless the agreement contains a clause allowing a landlord to increase the rent s/he can only do so if:

- the tenant agrees to any increase
- they have a statutory right to increase the rent (see below).

If there is a clause allowing the rent to be increased (often termed a rent review clause) a student should be advised to read it carefully and if necessary have it checked legally. They should think carefully before signing the agreement if they are unhappy with anything it says about increasing the payable rent.

Today, most students have **assured shorthold tenancies** (ASTs). In the case of an AST, the landlord will not be able to increase the rent in the first six months of the tenancy, or (if it is a fixed-term tenancy) for the duration of the initial fixed term. After this, it all depends on whether the student simply carries on in possession, or whether they sign a new agreement. In the former case, the rules are much the same as for **assured tenancies**. In the latter case, they are bound to pay the rent requested in the new agreement.

In the case of assured tenancies (see Chapters 1 and 10) it is possible that there will be a rent review clause allowing rent to be increased even during the initial period of the tenancy (ie before the end of any fixed term). Always encourage students to check for this.

A landlord's right to increase rent depends on whether the tenancy is **fixed term** or **periodic** (see Chapter 5). If it is fixed term, the rent cannot be increased until the fixed term expires, and a statutory periodic tenancy (see Chapter 10) comes into being (section 13 of the Housing Act 1988). If it is periodic, the rent can be increased by the service of a notice by the landlord under section 13 after one year has passed from the beginning of the tenancy.

The procedure a landlord has to use to increase rent under section 13 is complicated but in outline they have to serve a **notice of increase** on a tenant (giving them at least one month's warning). If the tenant is unhappy with the proposed increase, they can refer it to the appropriate local **residential property tribunal** (RPT). The RPT is usually made up of three people – a lawyer, a property valuer and a lay person. In the case of a section 13 notice of increase, their job is to decide whether the increased rent proposed by the landlord is in line with what would generally be expected in the area.

A person should always get advice before making an application to the RPT. It may be possible to be legally represented before the committee.

All the above assumes that there is no rent review clause in the original tenancy agreement. If there is one, it takes precedence over anything in section 13(1)(b)). Also, if a landlord persuades a student tenant to voluntarily accept a rent increase, this is legally binding (section 13(5)). So they should think hard before agreeing to any such proposal, and take advice if they have doubts.

There are no distinct statutory rules concerning **licences** and **non-assured tenancies**. Everything depends on what is stated in the agreement. If, for example, there is nothing in the agreement on increasing licence charges, it is safe to assume they cannot be increased for the duration of the agreement.

As regards council tenancies, local authorities have very wide powers to review rents regularly and impose 'reasonable' charges. Challenging this is a difficult and uncertain process. Anyone affected should seek advice first.

In the rare situation today that a student tenant has a **Protected** or **Statutory Rent Act Tenancy** (see Chapters 1 and 10) a landlord's ability to increase rents is very tightly controlled by law. Students are unlikely to have such a tenancy as, in general, a person needs to have to have been continuously in possession of their property since before 15 January 1989 to qualify. Space does not permit a full examination of the complex issues of rent and Rent Act tenancies – it is important to seek advice.

Challenging the rent

If a student is unhappy with a proposed rent, the obvious advice is not to enter into the agreement. In general a tenant is bound by the rent once they have signed. This is definitely the case with **non-assured/non-secure tenancies, licences, council tenancies** and **assured tenancies**.

As regards assured shorthold tenancies (ASTs), a person can, in theory, apply to the residential property tribunal (RPT) at the beginning of their tenancy if they think their rent is excessive compared to rents on similar properties in the area. The RPT will only decide to change the rent if there are enough ASTs in the area with which to compare it, and they think the existing rent is considerably higher than rents for similar properties (section 22 of the Housing Act 1988). There is no right to apply to the RPT concerning any 'follow up' ASTs. If the AST began at any time from 28 February 1997 onwards, a tenant has a right to apply to the RPT during the first six months of the tenancy (section 22(2)(aa) of the Housing Act 1988).

If someone is considering referring their AST rent to the RPT they should bear the following points in mind:

* The RPT will only reduce the rent if it is clearly excessive. The student should check with other students they know who live in similar properties in the same area.

* An assured shorthold tenant has very limited security (see Chapters 1 and 10). The landlord could decide to evict the student lawfully when their tenancy agreement ends if they chose to challenge the rent.

* If the student likes the property and would like to continue to live there when their current agreement ends, they have to consider whether challenging the rent is worth it, even if it does seem a little high.

If a person thinks they have a Statutory Rent Act or Periodic Tenancy they should take advice immediately. The rent is subject to strict statutory 'fair rent' controls via the Rent Officer and Rent Assessment Committee.

The obligation to pay rent

A tenant's principal obligation is to pay their rent (or licence charge) as and when it becomes due. If they fall into arrears, they become liable to eviction, even in cases where otherwise they have legal security. In general, rent arrears are not automatic 'grounds for possession' (see Chapter 10). Before a person is vulnerable to a rent arrears 'ground', the rent must be 'lawfully due'. In part, this relates to the relevant legal date for arrears to be outstanding (see Chapter 10) but also concerns the obligation of a landlord to give their tenants an address at which notices (including all legal notices) need to be served on them. If a landlord fails to provide this, rent is not regarded as being 'lawfully due' (see section 48 of the Landlord and Tenant Act 1987). If a landlord has not given the student tenant their name and address, they will not be able to enforce any rent demands against them. The address will typically be found in the tenancy agreement, or in the rent book if there is one.

Problems which can arise in relation to (claimed) rent arrears include:

- The landlord may refuse to accept any rent from the student tenant(s). This is most likely to arise if there is a dispute between them. To protect themselves in such a case, the students should write to their landlord stating they wish to pay the rent. A copy of this letter should be kept. They should then set up a bank or building society account and pay their rent into it, so they have the money to pay when their landlord eventually agrees to accept it (or takes them to court on grounds of rent arrears).

- A tenant does not have an automatic right to withhold rent if their landlord does not carry out, or refuses to carry out, repairs on the property. However, they may be able to do the repairs themselves and deduct the cost from future rent (this is discussed in more detail in Chapter 8).

If a tenant leaves the property before the end of a fixed-term tenancy or licence where there is no right to terminate early, or fails to give appropriate notice to quit or terminate the agreement even in cases (fixed term or periodic) where they can terminate early, they are legally obliged to pay rent until the end of the fixed term or the point when adequate notice would have expired. (The mechanics of giving notice are discussed in Chapter 10.) Even after a person has physically left the property, they still owe this unpaid rent to their ex-landlord as a debt and can be sued for it in the county court. If a landlord re-lets the property and another tenant or licensee enters into an agreement to move in, the ex-tenant's liability ends at that point.

A student should try to avoid 'walking out' on an agreement owing rent. Even if they find living in the property difficult, they should be advised to try to negotiate some kind of compromise with their landlord rather than simply leaving.

If a person is a joint tenant (see Chapters 5 and 6), they are liable for the whole rent due on the property, in conjunction with the other joint tenants. If one of the joint tenants leaves early owing rent, the landlord can choose to require those remaining to cover the sums outstanding rather than go after the tenant who has left. If a student finds themselves in this situation they can in theory seek recompense from the joint tenant who left, but this is legally difficult and they should always seek advice.

- If a student leaves the property still owing rent to their landlord they will, in practice, be able to keep back any part of their deposit corresponding to the rent owing. It is debatable whether it is technically correct to view unpaid rent as payable from the deposit. However, if a student sues their landlord for the return of their deposit (below) the landlord could in return sue them for unpaid rent (this is called a **counterclaim**).

- If the student moves out leaving unpaid bills for water, gas, electricity or telephone, it will generally be up to the relevant company to pursue them (if they are the ones named on the agreement with them) and possibly other users. The landlord should not deduct money from their deposit to cover bills unless the bills remained in their name or they suffered other financial loss as a result, for example in having to pay for services to be reconnected. In this type of case the student should seek advice.

Council tax

A full-time student living in a property where all the residents are students, or a student living in a hall of residence, is not liable to pay council tax (these are 'exempt dwellings'). A 'full-time student' in relation to council tax, means someone undertaking a full-time course of further or higher education.

Therefore, a student will probably not have to pay council tax (although it may be necessary in the case of private sector accommodation to ensure that 'exemption' is acknowledged by the council). The student may need to send them exemption certificates for all occupants – which should be obtainable from their university/college. However, given that liability will sometimes arise, the nature of council tax is summarised here. (This summary should not be taken to be a comprehensive statement of the law.)

* Council tax (which replaced the community charge, or 'poll tax' on 1 April 1993) is a tax on residential properties (referred to as 'dwellings'). It is the means by which local people pay towards the cost of providing local services, such as street cleaning, refuse collection, education and social services.

* There is one council tax bill for each dwelling but a number of people may be responsible for paying it (for example resident joint tenants).

* Liability for the tax arises on a daily basis.

* All dwellings are placed in one of eight valuation bands according to their assumed market value (nine bands in Wales). The lower the valuation band, the lower the council tax.

- 'Dwellings' includes houses, flats and bed-sits, whether lived in or not. It can even include houseboats and mobile homes.

- In addition to wholly student occupied properties and halls of residence, there are other 'exempt dwellings', for example an unoccupied dwelling vacated by a 'liable' person living elsewhere to attend college/university, and dwellings which are exempt for up to twelve months, for example a largely unfurnished dwelling which has undergone major repairs or structural alterations.

Situations where students may be liable for pay council tax:

- Where they are part-time rather than full-time students.

- Where the dwelling they live in is not wholly occupied by students. This can cause difficulties, particularly where a student leaves part way through a year (perhaps because they have left their course) and is replaced by someone who is not a full-time student. In theory, this tenant is then the one subject to council tax liability – the property no longer being exempt per se – but the situation can be confusing and the issue should be raised with the council immediately (there is a 25 per cent discount if only one person is 'eligible' as a 'non-student').

If a student feels that they may be in this kind of situation they should always take advice.

Consequences of the dwelling ceasing to be exempt

Council tax is potentially payable by all those residents in the dwelling. There is, however, a 'hierarchy' of liability. In order of priority this includes:

- a resident owner

- a resident tenant

- a resident sub-tenant

- a resident licensee

- if there is no one resident, the owner of the dwelling (although various discounts and exemptions will apply).

In addition, if a property fits the definition of a house in multiple occupation (HMO) – see Chapter 3 – then the owner is normally liable (a further practical reason why multi-occupied student accommodation might not, in any event, 'attract' council tax liability on the tenants).

A licensee (see Chapter 5) will only be liable to pay if there are no tenants or sub-tenants residing in the same dwelling. If there are a number of residents with the same status, they are jointly liable.

The main implications of this for students who are not exempt seem to be that:

* if they share the accommodation with their landlord (or the property is an HMO) the landlord is liable, not them

* otherwise as tenant(s) they are liable rather than any sub-tenants or guests (licensees) that might be living with them.

However, if they are joint tenants they are jointly liable. Also, even if they have individual tenancies, if they are all resident in the same house or flat, they appear to be jointly liable for council tax purposes. Any full-time student who has left their usual main residence to study elsewhere but retains owner-occupier or tenant rights over it should have this property exempted from council tax liability as well.

Council tax benefit

As its name suggests, council tax benefit (CTB) helps people on low incomes pay their council tax. The rules relating to eligibility for CTB are detailed and complex and, given that most students do not qualify, they are only summarised here.

Anyone who has to pay council tax and whose income does not exceed certain limits can get CTB, although there are some difficult cases, for example, 'persons from abroad'. As full-time students are not normally liable to pay council tax, the issue of claiming CTB does not usually arise. However, given that sometimes students are liable to pay, the question of whether they can claim CTB can be important.

Are students eligible for council tax benefit?

Full-time students are generally excluded from entitlement to CTB (see regulation 45 of the Council Tax Benefit Regulations 2006). In general it is irrelevant whether they receive any kind of grant or other financial support.

It can be difficult in some cases to decide whether a student is full-time or part-time. There is also some difficult case law (primarily in relation to eligibility for Income Support and Job Seeker's Allowance, where the same rule applies). At its simplest, someone is a full-time student if they are undertaking a full-time course of study. In the case of non-higher education courses, this generally means courses of more than 16 hours per week of guided study. In the case of higher education courses, it is necessary to examine the specific programme of study involved. There may be particular difficulty with modular courses that do not specify whether they are full-time or part-time.

If the university/college allows a student to interrupt their course temporarily because they are ill, or caring for someone, during this period they should not be regarded as a full-time student.

Otherwise, once someone begins a full-time course of study they are treated as a student until the last day of the course (unless they abandon the course or are dismissed from it early). If a student simply interrupts their course for personal or academic reasons, they are normally still deemed to be a student during this time even if they have little or no contact with the college and receive no financial help in their capacity as 'student'. Whether someone is a full-time or part-time student can be difficult to decide. A detailed treatment of these complex issues is beyond the scope of this book.

The main categories of full-time students who can claim CTB are:

* students under 19, who are not following a course of higher education

* students aged 60 or above, or whose partners are

* students in a couple where their partner is also a full-time student and either of them is responsible for a child or young person

- students who qualify for a disability premium
- students who have been incapable of work for 28 weeks or more
- lone parents
- students in receipt of income support, or income-based job seekers allowance (a student's eligibility for these benefits is also restricted).

In such cases it becomes necessary to calculate what CTB may be payable (the following should only be taken as an outline guide).

In general, CTB is calculated by assessing the whole of a claimant's weekly eligible council tax, then reducing this figure in line with the deductions laid down if there are any non-dependants living with the claimant. Non-dependants are usually adult children or other relatives or friends who live in the claimant's household on a non-commercial basis. The deductions represent the amount it is assumed such non-dependants will contribute towards the claimant's council tax, but they are implemented whether the person actually contributes or not. Situations where no deductions are made include those where the non-dependants are on Income Support or Income-based Job Seeker's Allowance, or are under 18, or are full-time students. As an example of the type of deduction otherwise made, if a non-dependant earns between £157 and £270.99 per week £4.60 is deducted from CTB entitlement (figure current as of April 2008).

After the non-dependant deduction has been made and assuming the person is not claiming Income Support or Income-based Job Seeker's Allowance, the CTB is reduced by 20 per cent which is in excess of the minimum laid down by law for a person to live on (known as their 'applicable amount'). This figure is affected if the claimant is a lone parent, if there are children, and if so how old they are, if the claimant has a disability and many other factors.

Non-dependent deductions in particular can be difficult and complex. If a student has a problem with them, or simply wants to check details such as the precise figures involved, they should consult one of the specialist books mentioned in Chapter 12, or take advice.

One of the trickier issues to arise in relation to student eligibility for CTB concerns the treatment of student loans (see regulation 51 of the Council Tax Benefit regulations 2006). All students who are eligible for a student loan are treated as being in receipt of one, whether they apply for, and receive one, or not.

A student loan is 'apportioned' over the period beginning in the first benefit week starting with the first week in September, or the first benefit week, the first day of which coincides with, or immediately follows, the first day of the autumn term (whichever is the earlier) and ending with the benefit week, the last day of which coincides with, or immediately precedes, the last day in June. The practical effect of this is to average out the loan as de facto income over a period significantly longer than a typical 'academic year' – around 42/43 weeks. This can be confusing, even for those students aware that a student loan counts as income. However, some loan income is ignored, for example:

* loans paid for tuition fees

* a fixed amount of £295 for travel expenses (2008/09 academic year)

* generally £10.10 of overall loan 'income' each week

* a fixed amount of £380 concerning books/equipment (2008/09 academic year).

Housing benefit

Even though most students do not pay council tax, nearly all of them pay rent or some equivalent payment for residential rights over the property they live in. Unfortunately, most students do not qualify for housing benefit (HB) to assist with the cost of this. Much of what has been said in relation to CTB also applies to HB:

* Full-time students on higher education courses are generally not eligible for HB (regulation 56 of the Housing Benefit Regulations 2006 treats such a person as if they were 'not liable to make payments in respect of a dwelling').

* Student loans count as 'income'.

* Non-dependant deductions are made.

* A number of groups of students are exempt from this, the rules being very much the same as for CTB (above).

The main difference between the HB and CTB calculations is that a student may not be eligible (even if they otherwise qualify for HB) concerning term-time accommodation if it is vacated during the summer. There are numerous exceptions to this. Advice should always be sought.

The income 'taper' for HB purpose is 65 per cent rather than 20 per cent. Before assuming that all rent will be covered by HB if a student does qualify for it, they should seek advice on issues such as the relevance of any non-dependants they may have living with them (see above), and how student loans are treated.

Case

Jan was a single mother with a young child. She was a part-time student at a college in the Midlands and rented a housing association property on an assured tenancy.

She contacted Shelter when her landlord took possession proceedings for rent areas. She had been in receipt of income support since her tenancy started four months ago and should have been receiving full housing benefit (HB) but the claim had not been processed.

Initially Shelter helped her to get the court proceedings adjourned for 28 days on the basis that her HB claim was outstanding. However, two months later the landlord advised that they were returning to court to seek a possession order, as the HB had not been paid.

The case was once again adjourned and the judge asked for a witness summons to be issued to the Housing Benefit Section.

Shelter contacted the Housing Benefit Section on Jan's behalf to advise them that a witness summons was going to be issued if the claim was not processed straightaway. The HB was subsequently processed, the arrears cleared and the possession order action halted.

Shelter also advised Jan to seek compensation for the distress and inconvenience caused by the HB delays, which had had a detrimental effect on her college work. This involved issuing a complaint to the Housing Benefit Section followed by a referral to the Local Government Ombudsman.

Jan and her son were able to stay in her home and the Housing Benefit Section eventually agreed to pay her compensation.

Rights and responsibilities for the property 8

Subjects covered in this chapter include...

Basic principles

What is the landlord responsible for?

What are the tenant's obligations?

Particular disrepair problems: dampness

Defective premises

What can the tenant do about disrepair?

Environmental health action

Statutory nuisance

The housing health and safety rating system (HHSRS)

Disrepair strategies

Basic principles

The standard of some student accommodation has improved over the last few years with the influx of companies specialising in building new student accommodation or renovating existing accommodation. However, there are still many students who are in rented accommodation at the cheaper end of the market. It is very likely that they will encounter problems with the condition of that accommodation. Even in some college accommodation, they may face problems and have to cope with older or cheaper furniture and equipment.

There is no reason why students should have to live in unsafe or unsanitary accommodation and many universities and colleges make substantial efforts to ensure good standards by imposing a code of standards on participating landlords.

There are also important laws and regulations that relate to these issues. In the case of gas supply and fittings, it is a criminal offence for a landlord to let accommodation without a current safety certificate (see Chapter 3), and other provisions cover electricity and fire safety.

In practice, the best time to attempt to resolve existing difficulties around disrepair and safety is before signing the tenancy agreement. After the tenancy has begun, the written agreement (if any) provides the starting point for determining who is responsible for what. Standard letting agreements usually indicate that the landlord is responsible for maintaining the main fabric of the premises, and the fixed installations to do with gas, water, electricity and sanitation. However, in virtually all cases the law imposes these obligations on landlords whether this is mentioned in the tenancy agreement and even if there is no written tenancy agreement at all.

The situation as far as responsibility for the state of decoration and supplied equipment can be more difficult to resolve as agreements may say nothing about them other than indicating that the occupier must not damage them.

Where it is established that the landlord is responsible, the major hurdle for many tenants is to get the landlord to carry out their obligations. Whilst this can be difficult in practice, ultimately students can sue landlords in the county court to make them carry out work or to pay compensation.

The local authority's environmental health service may be able to help. In some situations, they have an obligation to act against bad landlords and have powers to act in other situations.

What is the landlord responsible for?

The starting point for working out a landlord's responsibilities is the **tenancy agreement**. This forms a contract between the student and the landlord. Breaking its terms can lead to the student being entitled to compensation from the landlord for the misery of living in poor conditions, and any additional costs the student has incurred as a consequence eg additional heating costs where the accommodation is damp. In extreme cases, it could also justify the student cancelling a fixed-term letting early and leaving, but the student needs to take advice in these circumstances.

Where the student has a tenancy of any kind, including a verbal agreement, the law imposes basic repairing obligations on landlords of residential property under section 11 of the Landlord and Tenant Act 1985. These apply to assured, assured shorthold, non-assured, non-assured college lets, council accommodation and even excluded tenancies. They apply irrespective of what the tenancy agreement says or even of the non-existence of a written tenancy agreement. However, they do not apply in the limited number of cases where occupiers only have a licence. Students with licences can still be protected by the Defective Premises Act 1972 and by environmental health provisions that do not differentiate between licences and tenancies (see below).

These obligations can only be excluded in what would be very unusual circumstances for student lets ie where:

* the tenancy started before 24 October 1961

* there is a lease for seven years or more

* the parties contracted out of these obligations. This can only be done by the landlord and tenant obtaining a special (and virtually unheard of) court order before the tenancy starts.

The landlord is obliged to keep in repair the structure and exterior of the dwelling house. This includes drains, gutters and external pipes.

S/he is also obliged to keep in repair and proper working order the installations in the dwelling house for the supply of:

* water

* gas

* electricity

* sanitation

* space heating

* heating water.

This includes basins, sinks, baths and toilets but not other fixtures, fittings and appliances that make use of the water, gas and electricity supplies eg a cooker or fridge.

These obligations extend to the shared common parts of a building eg hallways and lifts, provided the tenancy started after 15 January 1989.

Where a landlord is responsible for repairs, any existing items that are defective must be repaired eg if the central heating was already broken or malfunctioning when the student moved in, the landlord is obliged to ensure that it works properly. The landlord would also be obliged to repair it if it worked when the student moved in but subsequently broke down. However, the landlord is not obliged to do things that amount to improvements. This usually means that the student cannot demand the installation of central heating if none was there when s/he moved in.

The landlord may also be liable for injuries caused through failure to carry out repairs (see below).

What are the tenant's obligations?

The law does impose some basic obligations on tenants. They are not responsible for repairing items damaged through wear and tear, but they must not deliberately damage the property. They are also obliged to behave in a 'tenant-like' manner. This means doing 'the little jobs about the place which a reasonable tenant would do' eg getting blocked sinks unblocked, replacing a fuse, and turning off water if they go away for a substantial period of time.

Case

A group of students went away for the Christmas vacation but did not leave the central heating on for a few hours each day, despite a specific clause in the agreement requiring them to do so. When they returned in January, pipes had burst, the property was completely flooded and all the ceilings had collapsed, rendering it uninhabitable. The students had to find temporary rooms with friends.

The landlord indicated he would carry out repairs as quickly as possible and the students moved back in after two months. It was agreed that no rent would be charged for this period and that the landlord would recover the cost of the damage from the students' deposits at the end of the tenancy.

Where a tenant wants to pursue a compensation claim arising from disrepair against a landlord, the claim could be reduced where the tenant has:

- failed to minimise damage caused by a disrepair by not promptly reporting problems to the landlord

- not stopped damage spreading (where it is possible).

Particular disrepair problems: dampness

Dampness can be one of the most problematic issues in rented accommodation. It may not be easy to work out what is causing the dampness and the landlord may not be wholly responsible in every situation. Dampness can be caused by condensation, construction processes or it can be rising or penetrating damp. The table below should provide some help in identifying and remedying dampness problems.

Identifying the problem: dampness

Possible characteristics	Damp patches on walls, damp smell in newly built or renovated property.	Bands of dampness and discoloration on ground floor walls up to a height of 18"- 36". Damp and/or rotten floor boards.	Patches of damp and/or mould eg in a corner of the ceiling, underneath the windowsill or on the walls. Crumbling plaster.	Condensation on windows, or puddles gathering on windowsills. Mould and dampness, or even drops of water, all over (usually) an outside wall. Can affect bedclothes near that wall or the contents of cupboards.
Type of dampness	Construction processes.	Rising damp.	Penetrating damp.	Condensation.
Cause	Plaster or concrete slabs not properly dried out.	Defective or absent damp proof course (DPC). Water logging of the surrounding ground due to inadequate drainage.	Faulty construction or lack of maintenance. Windows and doors that don't fit, holes in the roof, old or inadequate pointing to the brickwork, faulty joints in concrete slabs, blocked or leaking gutters, etc.	Warm moist air meets cooler wall surface or windows. Inadequate ventilation, insulation, heating and/or poor building design.
Remedy	Drying out.	Repair or insertion of DPC.	Repair fault, replastering.	Increase insulation, ventilation and/ or heating.

Condensation is generally not regarded as falling within the definition of disrepair unless it has caused damage to the fabric of the building. Whilst mould itself is not disrepair, if the dampness results in damage to plaster or woodwork, this will need repairing by the landlord. However, the repair may not deal with the causes of the condensation problem that could recur. Nevertheless, it is very likely to constitute a statutory nuisance and action can be taken by the local authority's environmental health service (see below).

Defective premises

In addition to the repair responsibilities of landlords under the tenancy agreement and section 11 of the Landlord and Tenant Act 1985, landlords can be liable to tenants for injuries caused by her/his failure to keep the premises in a safe state of repair. This arises under section 4 of the Defective Premises Act 1972. This will be the case provided the landlord is responsible for repairs. This does not necessarily get repairs done, but can give the tenant compensation if an injury results from a failure to carry them out. The landlord is liable if s/he knew or ought to have known of the defect that caused the injury. It is thus not always necessary for tenants to prove that they had notified the landlord of the defect before the injury was caused.

What can the tenant do about disrepair?

In the first case, the most important thing is to make a formal request in writing for the work to be done and keep a copy. Set out what needs attention and give the landlord a reasonable period to do the work. How long this is will depend on:

* how much work is required

* how seriously the disrepair is impacting on the student.

Many colleges, local authorities, registered social landlords and reputable private companies have scheduled repair periods for different types of repair eg 48 hrs for emergency works, one to two weeks for essential works, etc.

Where the student feels the landlord has failed to respond adequately, the student could seek assistance from the college accommodation service, a Shelter adviser or a citizens advice bureau, or a solicitor. Law schools in some universities operate free advice services run by supervised law students. They may be able to successfully negotiate on the student's behalf to get the repairs done.

Some local authorities run local arbitration or mediation schemes that may be able to effect a resolution to the problem.

In practice, the majority of disrepair cases are resolved through negotiation but if this does not work, the student has four possible courses of action to consider:

- give up the accommodation

- get the repairs done and claim the money back from the landlord

- take legal action against the landlord

- get the local authority's Environmental Health Service involved.

Giving up the accommodation

If it is near the end of term, the student may put up with the problem until s/he leaves. If there is other (better) accommodation available, s/he might want to leave. If so, s/he will have to follow the guidelines in Chapter 10. If the student does leave, the college accommodation service should be informed about the problem so they can consider removing the accommodation from their lists.

Getting the repairs done

Since the 1971 court decision in *Lee-Parker v Izzett*, it has been possible for tenants to get repairs done where landlords won't or don't do them. This is on the basis that the tenant organises and pays for the repairs and then deducts the cost from the rent.

The procedure

Tenants need to carefully follow the guidelines set out in the case. This means the tenant should:

1. Inform the landlord in writing of the repairs needed and ask for them to be done. It is a good idea to take photographs of the disrepair problems and send them too.

2. Allow the landlord a reasonable period of time to get the work done.

3. If the work is not done, the tenant should get at least three estimates for the cost of the work. Send copies to the landlord with a letter giving a further time limit for the work to be completed, failing which the tenant will get the work done themselves.

4. If landlord still fails to carry out work, the tenant can instruct the person who submitted the lowest estimate to do the work.

5. After the work has been completed, the tenant pays the bill. Make sure the student get receipts for work done and materials bought.

6. Send a copy of the bill and receipt of payment to the landlord to pay. It is best to use recorded delivery.

7. If the landlord does not reimburse the tenant, the tenant can deduct the cost from future rent payments. The tenant must restart paying rent to the landlord once the bill has been recovered.

Issues to bear in mind before going any further

* The student must be sure that these particular repairs are the landlord's responsibility.

* Remember deducting rent may not cover the cost of any improvements.

* This will only work if the student can afford to pay the bill for the repairs once they have been completed.

* If the bill is high, this is committing the student to stay for some time to recover the money spent.

* The student will technically be in rent arrears and the landlord may respond by trying to evict her/him. If, for example, the student is an assured shorthold tenant staying on after a fixed-term agreement ended, the landlord may respond by seeking to evict her/him simply by giving eight weeks' notice rather than on the basis of rent arrears (see Chapter 10). However, the student

should have a good defence to any such claim, in that s/he has been using rent money to discharge what would otherwise be the landlord's obligation.

* The cost is deductible from future rent payments, not rent arrears. In particular, the student cannot withhold rent to save up for the repairs. However, if rent arrears have accrued and a landlord takes court action claiming those arrears, it may be possible to ask the court to offset the arrears against the cost of the repairs – even if they have not been carried out. Provided the repair costs exceed the rent arrears, this could cancel out the landlord's claim. This is an issue where the student should get legal advice before defending the legal action.

* The tenant is responsible for the work carried out. If it is done poorly or negligently, s/he will be held accountable.

* It is crucial to keep copies of all the letters, estimates etc.

Taking legal action

Before issuing any legal proceedings in court, the student needs to be aware of what the landlord's response might be. If the student has little or no security, the landlord may try and evict them. (Chapter 10 looks at how landlords can legally seek to evict tenants. It is essential for the student to seek legal advice before issuing legal proceedings in court.)

The law recognises the difficulties in taking legal action on disrepair by having a different threshold for small claims in the county court than for other cases. If a disrepair claim is for less than £1,000, it is dealt with as a small claim. This means that a tenant does not normally have to pay the other side's legal costs even if they lose the case. Of course, it also means that the student cannot recover legal costs if s/he wins the case. Where a disrepair claim is for more than £1,000 however, it may be dealt with as a mainstream case by the county court. This means that claimants may be eligible for **public funding** (formerly legal aid) to employ a solicitor for these cases.

There are two main kinds of remedy that the tenant can seek:

* **an order of specific performance** – this is an order that the landlord must carry out specific repairs

* **damages** – this is a payment from the landlord to compensate for the losses the student has suffered as a result of the landlord's failure to carry out the repairs.

Damages can cover payment for things such as:

* physical discomfort suffered

* inconvenience caused

* not being able to use part of the accommodation

* the cost of alternative accommodation if the conditions were so bad the student was forced to move out

* the costs of redecoration or cleaning up

* damage or injury to the student's health

* work the student had to carry out

* damage to the student's belongings

* the costs of purchasing heaters where the landlord failed to repair existing heaters.

Where legal action is based on a landlord's failure to comply with their contractual repairing obligations, it is important to have:

* written evidence of when the student complained to the landlord about the problems

* evidence of the amount of money the student has spent to back up a damages' claim.

The general rule is that a landlord's liability does not arise until s/he is given notice of the disrepair and has failed to carry out the repair within a reasonable time. Notice is not necessary where the landlord actually knows about the problem. How long the reasonable period of time in which the repair must be carried out is a question of fact and degree dependent on its seriousness and the impact on the tenant of the disrepair.

The landlord receiving notice is crucial to the calculation of a damages claim. Providing evidence of the notice can be difficult. The obvious action is to phone the landlord or the agent but it is important that the student sends the landlord a letter that describes the problem and ideally photographs which show the problem. The letter should be dated and a copy kept.

Launching a counterclaim

Where a landlord initiates legal proceedings against a tenant that includes a money claim (for example, for rent arrears), the tenant may be able to successfully counterclaim where the landlord has failed to properly maintain the accommodation. This could result in the landlord's claim being offset against the tenant's counterclaim. Some tenancy agreements may seek to forbid the tenant from making any 'deduction or set-off' against the rent. However, the Office of Fair Trading's guidance suggests that such a clause is unfair and that the tenant's deposit provides a security for the landlord if the tenant doesn't comply with the tenancy agreement (*Guidance on Unfair Terms in Tenancy Agreements*, p78).

Environmental health action

All local authorities have Environmental Health Officers (EHOs). Many have environmental health departments though their titles may vary slightly. The authorities have a wide variety of statutory duties and powers that relate to housing. They are under a duty to take some action if the student's accommodation constitutes a 'statutory nuisance' or in some cases, is a health or safety hazard. They may decide to take a number of courses of action to deal with the student's problems in other situations, or where it constitutes a house in multiple occupation (HMO). Where EHOs have discretion about taking action, some are quite proactive while others show a marked reluctance to act because of the resource implications.

Licensing of HMOs

Chapter 3 looks at the requirement for some HMOs to be licensed by the local authority. Where a licence is required, it may be revoked if the landlord contravenes any housing or environmental health provisions or landlord and tenant laws that lead to civil or criminal proceedings resulting in a judgment being made against her/him. The tenant should check with the local authority whether the accommodation is, or should be, licensed.

Statutory nuisance

Premises are a statutory nuisance where they are in such a state that they are 'prejudicial to health or a nuisance'. Prejudicial to health is defined as injurious or 'likely to cause injury' to health. The concept has recently been described in court as applying to filthy or unwholesome premises likely to cause disease or illness.

The following are likely to be statutory nuisances:

- blocked drains or toilets
- leaking roof
- loose banisters
- piles of rubbish
- dangerous wiring
- broken lavatory
- serious dampness (including condensation related dampness)
- dangerous structures.

A defect could be a statutory nuisance if it is a danger or nuisance to neighbours or passers-by eg:

- serious damp coming in from next door
- tiles falling from the roof onto the street
- rotten window frames which might fall out.

Complaints made about poor housing conditions must be investigated by EHOs where they constitute a 'Statutory Nuisance' under the Environmental Protection Act 1990. Where an EHO is satisfied that a statutory nuisance exists, they must serve an **abatement notice**. This requires the landlord to end or remove the nuisance within a specified time. Non-compliance with the notice is a criminal offence. EHOs can then prosecute the landlord in the local magistrates' court. It can also undertake works in default and recover the cost from the landlord. Where a defect is of a structural character, notice must be served on the owner of the property.

There is a right of appeal to the magistrates' court against an abatement notice (within 21 days of service). The Secretary of State for the Environment has made regulations about the circumstances in which notices may be suspended pending appeal and specifying grounds for appeal.

It is possible for tenants themselves to take out a private prosecution against a landlord though this is only likely to be necessary where an EHO refuses to act or where the landlord is the local authority itself. The student needs legal advice before doing this.

Magistrates' court hearings regarding statutory nuisance

If the magistrates are satisfied that a nuisance existed at the date the legal proceedings started, the person taking the action is automatically entitled to costs (expenses) even if the nuisance ended or abated before the court hearing. If they are satisfied that a statutory nuisance still exists, they must make a nuisance order requiring abatement and may impose a fine. If a nuisance is 'likely to recur', the court can make an order to carry out repairs to prevent a recurrence.

Compensation

Under the powers of the Criminal Courts Act 1973, the magistrates' court can make a compensation order for up to a maximum of £5,000 for 'any personal injury, loss or damage resulting from' the offence. While the courts have said that compensation orders are appropriate where a civil court could not award damages ie because there was no strict disrepair liability, they have also said that:

- substantial awards should not be made where the tenant could recover damages from the landlord in civil proceedings (especially for personal injury)

- compensation should be calculated from the date the abatement notice was issued to the date of conviction (ie it does not cover the whole period of the nuisance).

The housing, health and safety rating system (HHSRS)

A new system for safeguarding occupiers' health and well-being came into force on 6 April 2006. It replaced the fitness for human habitation rules that had previously existed. The HHSRS focuses on dealing with the health and safety hazards that may arise through poor housing conditions. Its operation is complicated.

The system focuses on the possible effects that a hazard in the property may have on the tenant. Hazards can fall within four possible groups: **physiological, psychological, protection against infection**, and **protection against accidents**. These are sub-divided into 29 potential hazards, including: damp and mould growth; excess cold; excess heat; asbestos; biocides; carbon monoxide and fuel combustion products; lead and radiation.

The most common hazards include lead in drinking water pipes and old paintwork, cold, fire, falls, and hot surfaces that could lead to burns or scalds. These could involve hazardous fires, heaters, cookers and hot taps. The damp and mould growth category covers the threat to health associated with the increased prevalence of house dust mites, mould, and fungal growth resulting from dampness and/or high humidity. It can also include threats to mental health caused by the presence of damp.

Where there is a potential hazard in the accommodation, an Environmental Health Officer (EHO) has to make an assessment of the seriousness of the risk attached to it. Risks must be rated as to whether they are likely to:

- be life threatening or to cause major injury

- cause significant injury

- cause minor injury – injury refers to physical and mental health.

The hazard risk is calculated by assessing whether these possible outcomes are inevitable, probable, possible, or unlikely within the next 12 months. The assessment is based on the risk to the potential occupier who is most vulnerable to that risk, not just to the actual occupier at the time. The calculation results in a mathematical score that is the major influence on the subsequent actions to be taken by the authority. Local authorities have a duty to deal with serious hazards that are assessed as 'Category 1' and discretionary powers to deal with less serious 'Category 2' hazards.

The range of enforcement options includes:

* Prohibition notices

* Emergency prohibition notices

* Improvement notices

* Emergency improvement notices

* Hazard awareness notices

* Emergency remedial action.

An example of a Category 1 hazard might be a gas water heater leaking carbon monoxide: the risk is high and the outcome could be death. In such a situation, the local authority has the power to remove the imminent risk of serious harm. Such intervention by the authority does not require a prior notice to be served, but an appropriate notice must be served within seven days of the start of the action. In such an emergency there is no need for the authority to obtain a magistrate's warrant to enter premises to carry out the work. A less serious hazard might be a missing stair spindle. While this could be a serious hazard for a young child, it would be less of a hazard for adult students.

Serious disrepairs could lead to the service of improvement notices requiring the landlord to carry out work or even prohibition notices that forbid tenants from living there.

Case

Ten students moved into a large house. They went to their university accommodation office as one had got an electric shock, and there was sewage leaking into the back yard from a soil pipe, so only one of three toilets was usable. The environmental health department of the local authority was contacted. They immediately declared the house unfit for human habitation, and served a seven day repair notice for the plumbing, electrical and other defects they found. After seven days the repairs had not been carried out, and the students were advised to find other accommodation. They were reluctant to do so as ten bedroom properties were rare and it meant the group would have to split up.

After further inactivity by the landlord, the local authority started proceedings and eventually the students realised they had to move out. The work was carried out by the local authority in default, and they persuaded the landlord to split the house into smaller flats. The landlord's properties were also removed from the local accreditation scheme, and the students consulted a solicitor who was successful in obtaining compensation.

Disrepair strategies

The student does not have to choose between taking legal action against the landlord or getting environmental health services involved, they can do both. However, the student needs to be aware of what each can achieve and their relative advantages and disadvantages. It would be worth taking advice from a lawyer and the local authority before taking action.

The advantages of the local authority taking environmental health action can include:

- the student may be able to persuade the landlord that they aren't 'causing trouble', thus reducing the risk of the landlord responding by seeking to evict

- the local authority takes responsibility for the legal action

- it doesn't cost the tenant anything

- it can deal with some problems that are not strictly covered by disrepair obligations eg condensation.

The disadvantages may be that:

* the standard of repair required may be just enough to deal with the immediate problem ie 'a patch', but does not resolve it in the long term

* the amount of compensation the student gets, if any, is likely to be very limited

* the student has no control over how the matter is resolved between the EHO and the landlord

* the whole process is more complicated where the local authority is also the landlord

* it can still take months to resolve.

The advantages of taking legal action based on a landlord's breach of the contract can include:

* the student initiates and has control over the action

* the student can claim compensation from the landlord to cover most of the losses suffered

* public funding (formerly legal aid) may be available to pay for a lawyer if the student's claim is for over £1,000.

The disadvantages may be:

* the legal definition of repair doesn't cover all poor housing conditions

* the student must be able to show that they gave the landlord notice that repairs were needed (though this need not be the case if the claim is based on the Defective Premises Act)

* it may take some time to resolve

* the student will need to pay a lawyer if s/he is not eligible for public funding

* it can be difficult to find lawyers to take on these cases

* the landlord may respond by seeking to evict the student.

Tenants' problems with neighbours

9

Subjects covered in this chapter include...

The legal concept of 'neighbours'

Noise

The landlord's position

What if the problem is something other than noise?

Harassment

Claims against tenants

Students in the community

Noise and disturbance from those living next door, or a generally bad and difficult atmosphere with co-occupiers, can be just as large a problem as the property itself being in a bad state, or having problems with the landlord. Much of the law about neighbours if far from clear-cut, so legal solutions (even where theoretically available) may make neighbour problems worse. This chapter looks at the law and legal remedies, and also considers a range of 'non legal' approaches.

The legal concept of 'neighbours'

'Who then in law is my neighbour?' – This quotation is taken from the judgment of Lord Atkin in *Donoghue v Stevenson* (1932). In it, Lord Atkin uses the concept of 'neighbour' as the basis of establishing liability in the law of Negligence. In effect, he states that everyone owes a duty to be careful to her/his 'neighbours'. He says that your 'neighbour' is someone likely to be 'closely and directly' affected by your conduct. In the housing context with which we are concerned, the law has generally used the word 'neighbour' in a more restrictive sense – generally those who live next door or (at least) nearby. However, Lord Atkin's wider use of the term may have relevance when considering relationships between occupiers in the same house or flat, and in particular, the responsibility a landlord might have concerning the behaviour of occupants of their properties.

In cases of noise or other disturbances, a 'neighbour' is generally the person occupying 'neighbouring' premises. This need not necessarily be the person immediately next door, but in practice it is likely to be someone living fairly close, as a person needs to be badly affected by the noise or other disturbances to have significant rights.

If the problem relates to harassment or intimidation, a tenant may have rights against the perpetrator whether they live in the same property, next door, nearby, or completely outside the locality. If a tenant believes that they are in danger of physical violence, they should contact the police. However, the ways in which a person can legally protect themselves or seek compensation may depend on where the perpetrator lives.

If the complaint is against the tenant, and they are being threatened with possible eviction as a result, they may have a problem if their conduct or that of anyone living with or even visiting them caused actual (or potential) nuisance or annoyance to anyone in the locality. Locality is not precisely defined in law but seems to mean the neighbourhood or area.

Noise

Noise is one of the most common complaints and sources of friction. People have greatly differing sensitivities to 'noise pollution'. The problem of noisy neighbours raises issues not only of what the law is, but also whether the use of legal sanctions is the most satisfactory way of dealing with things.

What is the law?

The control of excessive noise is mainly through two separate areas of law – the common law tort of private nuisance and the 'public' controls imposed by the Environmental Protection Act 1990 and the Noise Act 1996.

A **tort** is what lawyers call a civil wrong, in other words it is not a criminal matter involving the police, but something that has to be resolved between those affected. At the heart of the tort is the idea that the person responsible for the nuisance had been behaving unreasonably. Private nuisance is usually defined as any unlawful interference with another's use or enjoyment of their property. A nuisance can be caused by unpleasant smells, smoke, the escape of water, and blocking off someone's light.

Noise nuisance is however, the most common example. Unfortunately, there is no simple test for deciding whether the noise caused by a person's neighbour is excessive. There are obvious cases – for example, music played at high volume repeatedly throughout the night – but in most cases there is scope for argument.

It is also possible for noise to be so widespread in an area that it amounts to a public nuisance, which is a criminal offence (eg an excessively noisy outdoor music festival). If that seems a possibility, further legal advice should be sought, preferably in conjunction with others affected.

The Environmental Protection Act 1990, section 79(1)(g) says that noise 'emitted from premises so as to be prejudicial to health or a nuisance' amounts to a statutory nuisance. No particular formula is specified by the legislation – on receiving a complaint about noise, a council has to use its own professional judgment about whether the level and repetition of the noise is excessive. Therefore, although complaining to the council and having it check noise levels may make sense, there is no guarantee that it will take the same view about how 'excessive' the noise is.

Night-time noise is often the real issue and here the Noise Act 1996 may apply. If it receives a complaint about excessive noise between 11pm and 7am, a council has to take 'reasonable steps' to investigate the complaint. Under the legislation, the noise will be 'excessive' if it exceeds permitted levels (which may be varied from time to time) as measured by an employee of the council. If a person is concerned about noise levels it is worth having the level checked by the council to see if it exceeds the maximum level permitted.

What steps can be taken?

The approach differs depending on whether the issue is private nuisance, or the Noise and Environmental Protection Acts.

A tenant may be able to resolve the problem her/himself by talking to their neighbour, who may not appreciate that their behaviour is causing a problem.

If attempts at amicable resolution fail however, the most common approach concerning private nuisance is to send a 'legal letter' to try to induce the offender to moderate their activities. Such a letter would most typically come from a solicitor but a similar effect might be obtained by a letter from the students' union welfare service or another advice agency (see Chapter 12).

If all else fails, a tenant can try to obtain an **injunction** against her/his neighbour. An injunction is a court order, which prohibits an activity or places curbs upon it. Therefore, it could prohibit the creation of noise at specified times, and/or place specified limits on noise levels (for an example of this, see *Kennaway* *v Thompson* (1980) in which the Court of Appeal granted an injunction to the owner of a house near a lake on which power boat racing was held that limited the use of the lake to certain days and to certain noise limits). However, all this could take a long time, could be expensive (public funding may not be available), and is not certain of success, particularly given the lack of precision about what level of noise is so unreasonable as to amount to a private nuisance.

Under the Environmental Protection Act 1990 the most likely response of the council will be to send out one of its specialist 'noise officers' to check the level of noise on a number of occasions. If as a result, s/he takes the view that the noise is 'excessive' and that, therefore, a statutory nuisance exists, the council is under a duty to issue an **abatement notice** requiring the noise level to be reduced. If the neighbour continues to make the noise despite the notice, they are guilty of an offence.

Under the Noise Act 1996 once a council has received a complaint about night-time noise it has to take 'reasonable steps' to investigate the complaint (most likely in the same way as under the Environmental Protection Act). If the noise exceeds the specified level, the council has the power to issue a **warning notice**. If the neighbour continues to make excessive noise after receiving such a notice, they are guilty of an offence. The receipt of a warning notice, like an abatement notice, can, in itself, be a fairly effective deterrent. If a tenant feels that trying to settle the issue with their neighbour amicably won't work, they should contact the council immediately rather than getting caught up in the uncertainty of a private nuisance dispute.

What if 'flatmates' are the real problem?

Legally, as well as practically, this is a problem. All of the law discussed above presupposes that the noise comes from neighbouring premises. Certainly a private nuisance, whether based on noise or any other disturbance, only exists if it comes from another building or another piece of land. The most recent case law on what is now the Environmental Protection Act 1990 (*National Coal Board v Neath Borough Council* (1976)) makes it clear that a 'statutory nuisance' must be either a private or public nuisance or 'prejudicial to health'. Therefore, the Environmental Protection Act only applies if the noise is from neighbouring premises, unless it is so distressing that it is affecting a person's health. The Noise Act 1996 is explicit that the noise has to come from 'another dwelling' (section 2).

If a student's flatmates (whether joint tenants or not) disturb them with their noisy nocturnal activities, a practical approach might be called for – either talking things through with them or, if this fails, a complaint to the landlord.

The landlord's position

Generally, the person liable in private nuisance is the person in possession of the premises, which normally means the tenant and not the landlord. This was confirmed in *Smith v Scott* (1973) where the claimants had to move out of their house because the problem family next door had made their life intolerable by noise and vandalism.

However, if those responsible for the nuisance are not tenants but only licensees or trespassers, possession of the premises is, in law, retained by the landlord. If a landlord lets to such people, knowing of their tendencies, or fails to take steps to control them while they are there, s/he may be liable in nuisance (*Lippiatt v South Gloucestershire Council* (1999)).

In very rare cases it might be possible to take action against a landlord in negligence, rather than in nuisance. A claim in negligence was rejected in *Smith v Scott*, on the basis that there was no duty to take care to choose tenants who would not cause harm to their neighbours (*Donoghue v Stevenson*). This aspect of the *Smith v Scott* case has been academically queried, although it was followed subsequently in *Hussain v Lancaster City Council*. Both *Smith v Scott* and *Hussain* involved councils with public housing duties and the courts clearly felt it would be an unreasonable extra burden upon them to impose a duty of care towards neighbours. It is not completely clear how far the same view would be taken of a private landlord who knew or suspected that the incoming tenants were potential troublemakers.

Nevertheless, before anyone embarks on a legal challenge they should be aware that such case law as there is, is generally against a landlord being liable.

A landlord can be liable if they have 'explicitly authorised' the nuisance while being aware of its nuisance-making potential. In *Smith v Scott* this principle was not applied, in part because the council had inserted a clause into the relevant tenancy agreement forbidding the tenants to create a nuisance. So they could not be said to have 'authorised' the subsequent conduct of the tenants.

Again, the law is not encouraging about actions against landlords – particularly as a significant factor could be the existence of a 'no nuisance' clause in the neighbour's tenancy agreement (which the other tenant will not have an automatic legal right to have access to).

Does it make a difference to the landlord's liability if the disturbances are being caused by a tenant's 'flatmates'?

As noted above, taking action against flatmates for noise and other disturbance is legally very difficult. It might, however, be worth a tenant complaining to their landlord. If they are in a joint tenant relationship with those causing the problem, or they are (in some way) part of the tenant's 'household', this could be a risky step since the tenant might be liable themselves for what the 'others' do (see below).

However, in some cases the landlord may be able to bring pressure to bear individually on the other(s) – in extreme cases by threatening, or actually taking, possession proceedings against them. Equally, there seems no way legally to force a landlord to act in this way.

Does it make any difference if the landlord is a university?

If a tenant occupies a room in any kind of hall of residence then it is likely that fellow residents in the hall will also have signed an agreement linking occupation of the hall to the university/college's general disciplinary regulations (for a full discussion of this, see Chapter 2). These regulations will probably contain specific sanctions concerning misbehaviour in hall, ranging from fines, to suspension or expulsion from university. Links to disciplinary regulations may also be found in 'head tenancy' and similar agreements (see Chapter 2) – but this is more variable in practice. Therefore, if the student is a victim of misbehaviour, complaining to the hall manager, warden or 'resident tutor' and ultimately the university accommodation service is likely to prove effective.

If a tenant's university landlord proves reluctant to act, it may be possible to put pressure on them via their department, academic tutor, or the students' union. Legally, the position of the university landlord seems much the same as other landlords and it is likely that the courts would be as reluctant to have extra burdens placed upon them to curb troublemakers or face legal liability as in the public landlord cases already mentioned.

Case

Complaints were made to the hall manager about Emma's boyfriend, Ken. He was staying with Emma frequently. He was unpleasant and aggressive towards the other students living on that floor and they suspected that he was stealing their food from the fridge. It was also rumoured that Ken was wanted by the police.

After two informal warnings by the hall manager, Emma was called to a formal disciplinary hearing as she was in breach of her licence agreement by having a semi-permanent guest. Ken had by this time been arrested and Emma was in financial trouble. She had made peace with the other students on the corridor and was given a final written warning for breach of house rules that formed part of the tenancy agreement.

Comment

This case emphasises the point that students need to be particularly aware that they can be held responsible for the behaviour of their guests.

What if the problem is something other than noise?

The law of private nuisance, with all its difficulties of enforcement, applies to a much wider range of activities than merely disturbance caused by noise. Examples of the wide range of 'unreasonable' activities seen to be nuisances include:

- allowing trees to overhang a neighbour's garden, or tree roots to penetrate the neighbour's property

- allowing a drain to become blocked so that the water flows onto a neighbour's land

- allowing offensive smells or smoke (eg from a factory) to drift over a neighbour's land

- allowing excessive heat to pass into a neighbour's property.

Equivalently, the Environmental Protection Act 1990, section 79 also covers a much wider range of 'statutory nuisances' than merely noise nuisance. Specific instances are:

- 'smoke emitted from premises so as to be prejudicial to health or a nuisance' (section 79(109b))

- 'fumes or gases' with equivalent effect (section 79(1)(c))

- 'any animal kept in such a place or manner as to be prejudicial to health or a nuisance' (section 79(1)(f)).

As with noise nuisance, if a person complains to the council about any of these matters, it will investigate their complaint but will form its own judgment as to whether intervention is required. In theory, if someone is unhappy with a council decision not to act, they can bring a court action themselves in the local magistrates' court (section 82). Before they consider taking legal action under the Environmental Protection Act 1990, they should always seek legal advice.

Harassment

Harassment can take many forms, ranging from nuisance telephone calls or emails, to serious intimidation by 'stalkers' or ex-partners. This book is specifically concerned with housing rights and many of the wider aspects of harassment are beyond its scope. However, as stated at the beginning of this chapter, in serious cases of harassment a student, like anyone else, should always consider contacting the police.

The Protection from Harassment Act 1997

Section 1 of this Act makes it a criminal offence to do anything that the perpetrator knew (or ought to have known) would be likely to amount to harassment of another person. The Act does not define 'harassment' although it does state that there must have been harassment on more than one occasion. However, it seems clear that the term covers not only threats and explicit intimidation, but also 'stalking', offensive and distressing telephone calls, emails and letters, and methods of debt collection which are humiliating and distressing. The word 'harassment' seems to imply something sustained and intended to annoy or distress.

In a housing context, if a neighbour deliberately intends to annoy or distress another person (perhaps because of some other dispute) by loud music or banging on the walls, they may have committed a criminal offence.

The existence of a criminal offence is probably the most important part of the Act, but by section 3, harassment also involves potential civil liability. Therefore, a tenant could try to curb their neighbour's future activities by means of an injunction (above) or in extreme cases, sue them for damages for the psychiatric harm they have caused.

If someone feels they are the victim of harassment, complaining to the police is normally the obvious step to take. However, they may also need to take legal advice about whether any civil remedies are also available to them.

Claims against tenants

So far this chapter has covered what can be done by someone who is the victim of bad behaviour by those around them. If they are the 'accused' much of what has already been said remains relevant, whether this relates to noise, some other nuisance, or more general harassment. In such a case, three distinct issues need to be considered:

* a tenant's vulnerability to being evicted
* the extent to which a tenant is liable for what others living with them do
* antisocial behaviour.

Unreasonable behaviour and eviction

Whatever a person's legal status in the property where they live (see Chapter 10), nuisance or other unreasonable behaviour can make them liable to eviction.

If they have legal protection as an assured or secure tenant the formula is the same, being based on their conduct 'causing or being likely to cause a nuisance or annoyance to a person residing, visiting or otherwise engaging in a lawful activity in the locality'.

In all cases it is merely a discretionary ground for possession, and re-possession is not automatic, although there is an increasing tendency for outright possession orders to be granted against 'repeat offenders'.

If a person is a periodic non-protected tenant or licensee, then a reason for seeking to evict them does not need to be given (although a court order will usually be required, see Chapter 10).

However, in practice 'bad behaviour' on a tenant's part will be a very common reason for their landlord to seek to evict them (not least because of the impact their behaviour might be seen to have on co-occupiers or neighbours).

If their non-protected tenancy is a fixed term one, it is common to find an 'early termination' or 'break' clause centring on nuisance or other unacceptable behaviour.

If a tenant is at risk of eviction because of (claimed) unreasonable behaviour, they should seek legal advice, particularly if they otherwise have some security in the property.

Liability for the conduct of others

A tenant is generally liable, both in the area of private nuisance, and in relation to eviction, for what their guests and visitors do. Also, all joint tenants (see Chapter 6) are liable for what other joint tenants do. However, individual tenants or licensees are not intrinsically liable for the misbehaviour of others living in the property who do so under separate licence or tenancy agreements, as they are not part of the same 'household'. If a person's tenancy or licence agreement is written so as to expressly make them liable for what such people do, the legal result is more difficult. This is quite common in relation to halls of residence, and quasi-halls run by private landlords in co-operation with universities. The view we, as authors, take in Chapters 2 and 5 is that such 'collective responsibility' clauses may be invalid as unfair contract terms. A similar view is taken by the Office of Fair Trading (OFT).

Antisocial behaviour

Making excessive noise, or creating other disturbances is clearly antisocial; but currently, 'antisocial behaviour' normally focuses on criminal activities that are a problem for the immediate community. If student tenants are subjected to this kind of accusation, there are a number of possible consequences:

* criminal charges against them

* the extreme likelihood (discussed above and in Chapter 10) that they will face eviction from the house or flat they occupy

* an injunction being taken out by the council against them, restraining their future activities in the locality

* an 'anti-social behaviour order' (ASBO) under section 1 of the Crime and Disorder Act 1998. Such orders last for a minimum of two years and could even involve a person's exclusion from the whole of the area of the relevant council. This would obviously have very serious

implications for a person's ability to continue with their course.

If there is a possibility of any of the above applying to a student tenant they should seek legal advice immediately.

Students in the community

Universities and colleges are coming under increasing pressure to intervene and mediate, or even use disciplinary regulations where students' lifestyles are a cause of friction within the area in which they live.

The issues here are much wider than whether individual students or even student householders are guilty of noise or other antisocial behaviour. In part, any problems are the product of the inevitable tensions caused by rapid environmental change and tolerance to differing lifestyles.

Therefore, instead of facing a direct complaint from a neighbour, or even legal action, a student may find that the university or college becomes involved. At worst they may find themselves charged under university disciplinary regulations. However, it is at least arguable that invoking university disciplinary sanctions about behaviour outside the university, short of criminal conduct, is intrinsically invalid. This is because the university is either acting 'outside its powers' or such a provision amounts to an 'unfair' term. The OFT does not, to date, appear to have made any 'rulings' here.

The use of disciplinary sanctions concerning alleged misbehaviour in the community is becoming more common. Its legality is open to question, although universities themselves would be very likely to invoke their responsibility to the wider community if challenged. However, it is clearly important for students to be aware of the need to be sensitive to neighbours who may have different lifestyles to their own.

Case

Adam, Brian, Colin, Darren and Eric rented a terraced house that was owned by an absentee landlord and managed by a letting agency. Complaints about noise were made by the adjoining owner/occupier at the start of the tenancy, both to the letting agency and the accommodation office of the university the students attended. It was alleged that loud music and foul language emanated from the house on more than one occasion in the early house of the morning, which was particularly distressing as the neighbour had three young daughters. Although the tenancy agreement was between the letting agency and the group of students, the university was sensitive to concerns about the relationships in popular student areas between students in private accommodation, and other local residents.

The university therefore wrote a general letter to the students outlining the complaints and the need to show consideration for neighbours. Subsequent discussions with the students and their parents revealed that only Colin was involved in these particular incidents and that the other tenants were absent.

Further complaints about noise were received from the neighbour in early December and graffiti of an offensive nature had appeared in the windows of the house. A university accommodation officer called to see the graffiti and spoke to the students about the noise issue. More complaints were received two weeks later from the same neighbour, including a fax sent during a disturbance at 4am. The neighbour could hear loud music and foul language, as well as doors slamming, banging and jumping, which had been preceded by shouting in the street. Complaints from two other residents were also received.

The university now faced a dilemma. It was not a party to the tenancy agreement, but had received detailed complaints about a group of students who did not seem to take heed of informal advice to show more consideration to their neighbours. The letting agency seemed unable or unwilling to take effective action. The university therefore decided to take disciplinary action in accordance with the university regulations that prohibited unreasonable and unruly behaviour.

A formal disciplinary hearing took place with regard to the students' behaviour. The panel heard details of the complaints as well as evidence from Darren, Adam, Brian, Colin and Eric. The panel found that the students had behaved unreasonably and imposed a penalty in accordance with the university regulations, which consisted of a warning as to future behaviour and a £25 fine. They paid the fine and there were no more complaints about the students' conduct for the rest of the tenancy.

Comment

This case highlights several issues – reluctance of owners or letting agents to deal with complaints, and how to deal with repeated behaviour which is causing a nuisance but is possibly not bad enough for the local authority environmental protection department to act upon. In this case, the students' behaviour clearly caused distress to the adjoining owner and his family on several occasions. The complaints were specific and detailed, and although it transpired that not all students were involved in all incidents, as a group they were jointly and severally responsible under the terms of the tenancy agreement. There may be some doubt as to whether university regulations should extend to behaviour off university premises and in the wider community. The imposition of a modest penalty appeared to have the desired effect on this particular occasion.

Bringing lettings to an end

10

Subjects covered in this chapter include...

The tenant's initiative

The landlord's initiative

The university or college landlord

The council landlord

The private landlord

Sharing with resident landlords

Assured and assured shorthold tenancies

Landlord's right of termination

Mortgage repossession

Succeeding to a tenancy

Accommodation that comes with a job

Registered social landlords (housing associations)

The tenant's initiative

Students sometimes think that they are free to leave rented accommodation at short notice if problems arise. However, in virtually all situations, a student who is a tenant will have to give some advance notice in writing to the landlord indicating that s/he wishes to leave. How long a period of notice depends on a number of factors, including whether the tenancy is fixed term or periodic, and what (if anything) is stated in the tenancy agreement. In the normal course of events, where there is a written tenancy agreement, this should provide the basic information about the period of notice needed. In practice, the situation may be negotiable if a landlord is amenable, for example the landlord may agree to a 'surrender' of the tenancy.

Agreements for a fixed period

If the tenancy agreement is for a fixed period of time eg six months or a year, the student is bound to continue with it until the end of the agreement period unless there is some provision in the agreement that enables the student to leave earlier, or the landlord agrees to a 'surrender' of the tenancy. In very limited circumstances, the tenant may be able to terminate the agreement because the landlord breaches the contract in a fundamental way, for example by refusing to accept responsibility for heating (see *Hussein v Mehlman*). Equally, a co-operative landlord can waive their right to notice, and let a tenant leave early. The student is contractually bound to pay the rent for the full period that s/he originally signed up to. If the student still goes ahead and leaves, s/he is highly likely to lose any deposit paid. In addition, the student is liable for the balance of rent due for the remainder of the agreement period though the deposit and any advance payments of rent should be offset against this. While the landlord is not under a legal duty to try to find a new tenant, if the property is relet before the original fixed period ends, the student's liability for future rent would come to an end as soon as it is relet. This whole process is more complicated where the landlord has insisted on the tenant handing over post-dated cheques for the whole period at the start.

Where there is a written agreement for a short-fixed period, it will be rare to find a provision that allows the tenant to end it early. However, a longer agreement may contain a **break clause**. This will specifically allow either the landlord or the tenant to end the agreement after a prescribed period has run eg six months into a one-year agreement. It will normally specify how a notice to end the agreement should be given (eg in writing and addressed to the landlord) and the notice period.

Periodic tenancies

Where there is no fixed-period written agreement, the tenancy will be periodic. This usually means it is weekly or monthly and continues from week to week or month to month until either party brings it to an end. This can be done by serving a notice on the other. There are two basic principles that govern the period of notice required:

- the notice has to be for at least one full rental period ie, a week or month
- the notice can only expire at the end of a full rental period.

So a tenant who does not share accommodation with the landlord and who pays rent on a calendar month basis on the first of each month, would have to give a minimum of one month's notice. However, in this example, the notice can only expire at the end of a complete calendar month. A notice given on the 16 June would in fact only expire at midnight on the 31 July.

In most circumstances, a tenant is required by law to give the landlord at least four weeks' notice (section 5(1), Protection from Eviction Act 1977). However, there is nothing to stop a landlord agreeing to accept a shorter period at the tenant's request. The only exception to the four weeks' rule is **excluded occupiers**. This will mainly affect students who share some accommodation with the landlord or a member of the landlord's family, provided the property is their only or principal home. If the student is a tenant, the notice period in this situation is calculated solely on the basic principles above.

Giving notice

The student should always give notice in writing and keep a copy. This can be done by letter to the landlord and does not require the use of any specific form. The student should ensure that her/his letter is dated and specifies the leaving date. They should check the agreement for any specific requirements eg an address where the notice should be sent. Although it may not be formally required, it is also sensible to use recorded delivery or signed for post to provide evidence should there be a dispute.

Flat sharers with divergent interests

The situation is more complicated where people are sharing accommodation and one wants to leave while others want to stay. It is important to be clear whether the occupants are joint tenants or not (see Chapter 2).

(a) The sole tenant leaves

If only one of the students is the tenant, they need to comply with the rules above. The notice period is calculated on the principles previously explained. If the sole tenant leaves, this will mean that the other occupiers will lose their accommodation. If they want to take over the accommodation after the sole tenant has left, they will have to negotiate a new agreement with the landlord. Alternatively it might be possible for the tenant to transfer the tenancy to them, though this can usually only occur with the landlord's permission.

If a new agreement is not made, the existing tenant needs to ensure that the other occupiers also leave and that they are given proper notice to leave. The other occupiers could fall into three alternative categories:

* Where they are sharing the accommodation with the student tenant and making payments to them, they are quite likely to be **excluded occupiers**. This means they are at least entitled to some notice that their own arrangements will be ending, although this does not need to be in writing (see below). (The student tenant here acts in the role of a private landlord to the other students.)

- Where the others have rented a self-contained part of the accommodation from the student tenant and the student does not share accommodation with them, they are the student's **sub-tenants**. The law does not allow assured and assured shorthold tenants to sub-let without the landlord's permission and if the head landlord becomes aware, s/he could take possession action against the landlord/student tenant. If the head landlord has not given permission, the sub-tenants would become trespassers after the main tenancy has ended.

- If the sub-tenants are there with the permission of the landlord, the sub-tenants would have the same status that the departing tenant had. If, for example, the departing tenant was an assured shorthold tenant, the sub-tenants would now become direct assured shorthold tenants of the landlord. Even where a specific request has not been made, or an agreement given by the landlord, there may be an implied granting of permission if the landlord knows of the sub-letting and continues to accept rent.

(b) One of the joint tenants wants to leave

Where the landlord has rented property to two or more students, the situation may arise that only one of them wants to leave. Joint tenants are jointly liable for the tenancy. This means that any one of them can be held responsible for the whole of the rent. Simply leaving does not end this responsibility. A landlord could try to recover rent owed by a tenant who had left from the remaining tenants. A departing joint tenant will want to ensure that their liability comes to an end and will want to get their deposit back. The situation is complicated.

The occupiers have four options:

- The remaining joint tenants could continue with the existing tenancy, making up the shortfall in rent between them. A leaving joint tenant who had contributed to a deposit paid to the landlord, would want their deposit back. The remaining occupiers could raise this between them with a view to recovering it from the landlord when the whole tenancy ends. Alternatively, the departing joint tenant will have to wait until the landlord returns the whole deposit.

- They could find someone to replace the departing joint tenant. However, it will not be possible to bring in someone to become a new joint tenant without the consent of the landlord. The landlord is not obliged to agree to any new arrangement. However, where a joint tenant has left and been replaced with the landlord's knowledge and without her/his apparent objection, the student should seek advice on the situation. It is possible that the landlord has lost her/his right to object and her/his behaviour may be taken as an acknowledgement of the new arrangement.

- It may be possible to bring in a new person who does not become a joint tenant but simply pays a share of the rent to the remaining joint tenants. The occupiers need to check the tenancy agreement to see whether this is permissible. Some include clauses that forbid the students from 'taking in lodgers'. Breaching this term could lead to eviction for everyone. Nevertheless, where someone moves in with the landlord's knowledge and s/he continues to accept rent, this may be taken as an acknowledgement of the new arrangement and stop the landlord from subsequently taking action.

- The remaining occupiers could seek to remove the departing tenant from the agreement and take over the tenancy on their own. They would then have responsibility for the whole of the accommodation and the rent. In effect, this would amount to a new arrangement that would need the agreement of the landlord.

It is important to note that where the tenancy was periodic, a departing joint tenant could end their potential liability by serving a valid notice to quit on the landlord to bring the whole tenancy to an end. She/he can do this without the knowledge or consent of the other joint tenants. This would of course result in everyone losing their accommodation. Any notice served will not have effect if it expires in the middle of a fixed-period tenancy, but will have effect where the tenancy is weekly or monthly, or has become one after a fixed-period agreement has expired. The notice period is subject to the rules already noted above. If a student is a joint tenant whose rights to remain in a property are threatened in this way and they want to keep the tenancy going, they should seek legal advice immediately. The European Court of Human Rights has recently decided that in exceptional circumstances, the remaining student may be able to challenge the eviction on a human rights basis. The issue will need to be reconsidered by the House of Lords before it is possible to be sure of the position in the UK. In any event, a human rights challenge is only possible where the landlord is a public body, such as a local authority or (perhaps) housing association.

(c) A sharer who is not the tenant wants to leave

If someone else is the tenant and the student pays them rent, the student is likely to either be a **non-assured** or **excluded occupier**. If the student shares some accommodation with the tenant, the student will be an excluded occupier. In either event, the student will have to give a specific notice period depending on any agreement the student has with the tenant or, in the absence of written agreement, one rental period's notice expiring at the end of a complete rental period. Non-assured tenants have to give a minimum of four weeks' notice to the tenant.

Case

In March, four students agreed to take the tenancy of a flat above a restaurant. In September, a week before the start of the tenancy, one of the students had to drop out as he had failed his re-sit exams, so the others sought advice. They were advised to make the landlord aware so he might be more flexible with rent demands. However valid the reason for one tenant wishing not to move in, it was explained to the students that as joint tenants they were responsible for renting the whole property, and that they should seek a replacement tenant.

Soon they were back at the accommodation office as the landlord, who also owned the restaurant, said he had a chef who needed a room quickly. They were concerned about the compatibility of the group, and liability for council tax, as the mixture of students and non-students meant the property would lose its exemption from council tax. They were advised that a fourth tenant could not be forced upon them, but they would still be liable for the rent whether or not they accepted the chef. The fourth tenant may not meet their preferences for a flatmate but might be better than no tenant at all. Eventually a fourth tenant was found via the accommodation office and he moved in two weeks after the start of the tenancy.

The landlord's initiative

Basic principles

If a landlord wants students to leave accommodation rented to them, two main questions arise:

- Will the landlord be able to recover possession and when?

- What processes and procedures are involved?

Whether the student has to leave is a complex issue, as the law protects occupiers according to the kind of landlord and the type of residential arrangement they have. In some situations, landlords have clear rights to recover possession provided they go about things in the right way. In other situations, occupiers can only be evicted against their wishes where they have broken the terms of the agreement and grounds for possession are proved in the county court. In broad terms, people who rent from local authorities and housing associations are more likely to have a higher degree of protection than those who rent from private landlords and colleges. However, even the date the tenancy started may be of significance thanks to periodic alterations to the law.

In virtually all cases, letting agreements cannot be ended without the landlord first giving the student some written notice. Even after the notice has expired, in many cases, the landlord will be committing a criminal offence if s/he then evicts the student without having obtained a possession order from the county court.

If the student has entered a fixed-term tenancy agreement, the landlord cannot usually end it early unless the student has broken one or more of their obligations (known as covenants) under the agreement eg by not paying the rent, or behaving in an antisocial way. However, the landlord will normally be able to terminate the letting at the end of the agreement period even where there is no default on the student's part.

In most cases where the student is renting on a weekly or monthly periodic basis, a private or university landlord will be able to end the arrangement without any fault on the student's part simply by giving her/him the appropriate period of notice to leave. However, it may still be necessary to get a court possession order if the student does not leave at the end of the notice period.

The university or college landlord

The kind of accommodation let by colleges can range from variants of halls of residence, to individual houses or flats. Protection for the student is determined by the residential arrangement s/he has. The letting agreement may describe itself as a **licence** or as a **tenancy**. However, the courts have held that the wording in the agreement in itself is not conclusive of the real nature of the relationship between the parties. The issue of exclusive possession is at the core of the legal distinction. This comes down to who is actually in control of the premises, the student or the college.

A letting in a hall of residence under a licence agreement of accommodation is usually regarded as a genuine licence agreement rather than a tenancy (see Chapter 2). This is because the college has overall control of the premises and therefore the student does not have exclusive possession of the room. The college retains rights of access to the room and staff may well exercise these rights by entering the room in the student's absence to provide cleaning or other services. In these circumstances, the relationship between college and student is governed by the licence. In serious cases, the agreement may allow colleges to ask students to leave after giving a short period of notice.

Even so, not all arrangements involving hall accommodation constitute a licence. Where no services are provided, the accommodation may be in reality more akin to managed flats than the traditional concept of a hall of residence. In these circumstances, the occupiers may have a tenancy.

Where the arrangement does involve the student having a tenancy, for example where there is a separate house or flat, the situation depends upon whether the college falls within a list of 'specified educational establishments'. All universities and institutions which provide further education or higher education are automatically covered by government regulations, along with a number of other specified bodies. The result is that the arrangement can then at best be regarded as an **educational non-assured letting** on the condition that kitchen and bathroom facilities are provided. Sharing the use of these facilities with other students does not stop a non-assured letting arising.

In order to evict the student, the college must give her/him a formal written notice to quit in a prescribed form. The student is entitled to four weeks' notice and unless s/he leaves voluntarily at that point, a court possession order must be obtained before eviction can take place. However, in deciding whether to grant a possession order, the court will only be concerned that the technical formalities of the notice have been complied with. No specific reasons for wanting to evict, such as not paying rent or causing a nuisance, need to be proved by the college in court to get the order. However, a student who stays until a court order is made, is almost certainly going to be held liable by the court for the college's legal and court costs.

The council landlord

Not many students are tenants of local housing authorities (councils). 'Ordinary' council tenants can have a high degree of security. However, a student's rights can vary according to the exact nature of the particular housing arrangement. In particular, councils can make specific student lettings with much reduced security. It should also be noted that a student who is living in property owned by a local housing authority but managed by a college or housing association, will be regulated by the rules applicable to those landlords, not the council.

The basic terms of the student's relationship with the council will be found in the tenancy agreement. This will explain the circumstances in which the student might be asked to leave. Nevertheless, this is subject to extensive provisions in the 1985 Housing Act (as amended).

The majority of people who occupy council property have **secure tenancies**. This includes joint tenants who have their names on the tenancy agreement. It may not include a situation where tenants share with other people in hostel type accommodation. If asked to leave, there is a requirement that the council serves a secure tenant with a **notice seeking possession**. This is a prescribed form that must specify the particular basis of the request to leave as well as giving a full explanation of why this particular basis is being relied upon. Subsequently, the council can only end the tenancy by proving this reason in a court. The law here is complex and advice must be sought after receipt of a notice seeking possession.

Although most lettings made by councils are secure tenancies, a letting made to a person specifically because they are a student can fall outside this category. For this to be the case, the council must have notified the student in writing before the tenancy starts, that this exception to the general rules applies (paragraph 10, Schedule 1, Housing Act 1985). The notice must indicate that the letting is to enable the student to attend a specifically named educational establishment. The tenancy will expire six months after the student's course finishes. The terms of the agreement are significant, as they may specify situations where the student might be asked to leave. In the absence of specific terms, the council will not need to show any particular reasons for giving the student notice, but s/he must be given a written notice to quit. S/he is entitled to a minimum period of four weeks' notice and, in addition, the notice period can only expire at the end of a complete rental period. If s/he does not leave at that point, the council must obtain a court possession order against the student.

Where the student letting exception does not apply but the student has been granted a tenancy within the last year, this may fall within the category of an **introductory tenancy**. These are probationary tenancies but not all councils use these so check the agreement to establish whether this is the case. The agreement should specify the circumstances in which the student can be asked to leave within the first year. It is also possible for a council to extend the introductory period for a further six months. After serving the student with a notice, the council cannot evict the student against her/his will without first obtaining a court possession order. Although the provisions of the legislation do not require the council to identify any particular reason for seeking to evict, the courts have decided that councils do have to give reasons. However this is a developing area of law and the student will need advice. As in most other situations where a court possession order is ultimately made against the student, s/he is likely to have to pay the court costs involved.

The private landlord

Landlords, other than local housing authorities and housing associations, are generally regarded as private landlords. A student or parent who rents a property and then lets out parts to other students is also a private landlord. In some situations, the student might be living in a property owned by a private individual or company, but managed by the student's university or college, or a housing association. In these cases, the rules applicable to the university, college or housing association will apply, rather than the rules for private landlords.

With most fixed-term tenancy agreements made since 28 February 1997, tenants cannot be forced to leave during the tenancy period unless they have broken the terms of the agreement. Once the tenancy period has expired however, the landlord does not have to provide any particular reasons for seeking possession. However, the student's situation can vary considerably depending on their particular arrangements. One of the most significant factors that can reduce the student's rights is where the landlord lives in the same property as the tenant.

Most students renting from private landlords now have **assured shorthold tenancies** and the rules for the termination of these tenancies are described below. The main exception to these rules in private accommodation is where there is a licence rather than a tenancy, or the student has a resident landlord, and these exceptions are also dealt with below.

Tenants and licensees

The issue of whether the student is a **tenant** or **licensee** (see Chapter 2) can be significant. Where the student has self-contained accommodation and the landlord has no real control of the premises or a right of access to the accommodation other than to inspect the premises, the student is likely to be treated as a tenant. This is the case irrespective of what the letting agreement says. Where a student is one of a number of occupiers and all their names appear on the tenancy agreement, they will be joint tenants. Sharing facilities such as a kitchen, bathroom and toilet with other occupiers apart from the landlord, does not prevent the student from being joint tenants.

Typically, arrangements that involve informal agreements with relatives (particularly if no rent is involved) or the provision of services such as room cleaning or meals, prevent a tenancy coming into existence. A flat or house share, which involves each occupier having a separate and direct agreement with the landlord where the landlord replaces departing occupiers, may be more indicative of a licence arrangement. This may also be the case where the agreement gives the landlord the right to move the student from one room to another provided this is not purely a notional right.

Genuine licence agreements

Where there is a genuine licence agreement, the student will be a **non-assured occupier**. The student could even be regarded as a non-assured occupier where s/he lives in a self-contained flat in a converted house, provided the landlord lives in another flat. However, this rule does not apply where the landlord lives in a separate flat in a purpose built block of flats.

As a non-assured occupier and in the absence of specific terms in an agreement, the landlord will not have to give any particular reasons for asking the student to leave. However, the student must be given a written notice to quit, and is entitled to a minimum period of four weeks' notice. If s/he does not leave at that point, the landlord must obtain a court possession order against her/him.

Sharing with resident landlords

Where the student shares some facilities with a resident landlord, the student is likely to be regarded as an **excluded occupier**. This scenario applies where the student shares virtually any accommodation with their landlord or a member of the landlord's family. This rule only applies where the property is the landlord or the landlord's family member's only or principal home. It is thus not possible for a landlord to keep some personal possessions in one room in a number of properties and claim to be resident in them all.

There is a fairly extended definition of 'family' for these purposes (see section 113, Housing Act 1985). Similarly, the sharing of most facilities counts for these purposes. The legislation indicates that it applies to any sharing apart from of an 'area used for storage, a staircase, passage, corridor or other means of access' (see section 31, Housing Act 1988).

Excluded occupiers are particularly vulnerable when asked to leave. They are entitled to a notice period where they have an agreement that specifies one, but it is not uncommon in these situations merely to have an oral agreement. The student will only be entitled to a notice period equivalent to the rental period (eg a week or month). If the student is a tenant, the notice period can only expire at the end of a complete rental period. If the student does not leave at that point, the landlord does not technically need a court possession order before evicting her/him, though advice should be sought to ensure no possible criminal offences are committed.

Assured and assured shorthold tenancies

Where the landlord is not resident, private tenancy lettings fall into two categories: **assured** and **assured shorthold tenancies** (ASTs).

There are a number of other situations where tenancies cannot be assured or assured shorthold, though it is unlikely they will apply to lettings involving students (Schedule 1, Housing Act 1988). They are:

- Premises with particularly low or high rents. Where the tenancy was granted after 31 March 1990, this covers the situation where the rent is less than £1,000 pa in London (£250 elsewhere) or over £25,000 pa. Where tenancies were granted before 1 April 1990, this is calculated by reference to the old rateable value rather than the rent. There may be situations where a student provides part-time assistance to a landlord in return for a reduced rental payment. An example would be where the student does jobs to support an older landlord. The actual rent paid is the significant figure for the purposes of rent limits, unless a specific figure has been allocated to the services provided. This would be the case where a higher rent was originally agreed and then reduced to make allowance for the services (*Barnes v Barratt* (1970)).

- Business premises protected by the Landlord and Tenant Act 1954.

- Licensed premises such public houses.

- Agricultural land or holdings.

- Holiday lets. Although landlords have used these in the past, they are very rare these days.

- Premises rented out by the Crown, local housing authorities, development corporations, fully mutual housing associations or the Housing Action Trust.

Since 28 February 1997, the majority of new lettings have been assured shorthold lettings. Unless the letting agreement replaced a previously assured tenancy agreement, it will only be an assured letting where the agreement specifically says so.

Most landlords letting to students use written assured shorthold tenancy agreements for a fixed period of time. It is still entirely feasible to have an assured shorthold tenancy agreement that is oral and not in writing, though the problems of interpretation are fairly self-evident.

To evict a tenant lawfully under an assured shorthold or assured tenancy, the law requires the landlord to serve notice on the tenant and, should the tenant refuse to leave, the landlord would have to obtain a court possession order. The law only allows landlords to recover possession on certain grounds that are set out in the Housing Act 1988 (see below). Assured shortholds are most commonly ended by using a special ground that simply involves giving the tenant two months' notice.

Assured shorthold tenancies: two months' notice and the accelerated possession procedure

The simplest way for a landlord to end an assured shorthold tenancy is to give the tenant a minimum of two months' written notice (section 21, Housing Act 1988). This is appropriate where the tenancy is periodic, ie simply runs from week to week, or month to month, but it is also necessary in order to end a fixed-term tenancy. Unless a notice of this kind is served at least two months before the end of a fixed term, the tenancy will continue on a monthly or weekly periodic basis. A fixed-term tenancy cannot be ended part of the way through by using this kind of notice.

As far as the notice is concerned, no particular form is required and no particular reason needs to be cited or proved. However, calculating the exact period of the notice can be complicated:

- If the notice is given at least two months before the end of a fixed-term agreement, it expires on the last day of the agreement.

- If the notice is given later than two months before the end of the fixed term, the expiry date is two months from the date of the notice.

- Where a tenant stays on after the end date given in the tenancy agreement has passed, the tenancy will convert from a fixed-period tenancy into a periodic tenancy. In the absence of a new agreement, it is likely to become a weekly or monthly tenancy depending when rent is payable and will be treated as a periodic tenancy.

* Where a tenancy is periodic as opposed to fixed term eg a monthly agreement, two months' notice must be given, and additionally, the notice can only expire at the end of a complete rental period.

If the tenant does not leave after the expiry of the notice, the landlord must issue possession proceedings in the county court. This can be done under the **accelerated possession procedure**. The procedure is relatively simple and can be carried out online. It is unlikely in most cases to involve a hearing in court. The court must grant a possession order provided the landlord proves that it was an assured shorthold tenancy and that the notice was valid. The court can postpone the operation of a possession order for up to a maximum of 14 days. However, this can be extended to an absolute maximum of six weeks where exceptional hardship would result from an earlier eviction. While exceptional hardship is not defined, a student may be able to make a claim where for example, important exams are imminent.

Restrictions on the use of the accelerated possession procedure

All landlords who let out properties under assured shorthold lettings and who take a deposit from a tenant, are required to follow the procedures set out in the **Tenancy Deposit Protection Scheme**. Provided a landlord has taken a deposit on or after 6 April 2007, the accelerated procedure for regaining possession requires her/him to provide evidence that a deposit has been safeguarded with a tenancy deposit scheme. Failure to do so means that a more time consuming and expensive possession procedure needs to be followed. There are additional penalties that apply for failure to use the system (see Chapter 3).

A significant number of lettings to students under assured shorthold tenancies are likely to be in houses in multiple occupation (HMOs). Some HMOs must be licensed with the local authority under parts 2 and 3 of the Housing Act 2004. If a licence is necessary, the landlord is required to attach a copy of it to the accelerated possession claim form or show

that an application for a licence has been made to the local
authority. If s/he fails to do so, s/he will not be allowed to use
this procedure. This is significant, as at the time of writing, the
number of applications for HMO licences has fallen short of
what local authorities estimate it should be. Tenants receiving
claims under the accelerated procedure should thus check
the register of HMO licences kept by their local authority (see
Chapter 3).

A court cannot make a possession order solely based on the
giving of two months' notice if that means the tenant is evicted
sooner than six months from the date the tenancy started.

Assured and assured shorthold tenancies: grounds of possession

Where the landlord is unwilling or unable to use the two
months' notice procedure or where the student has an assured
tenancy, s/he might alternatively seek to end the tenancy on
the basis of one of the grounds of possession set out in the
1988 Housing Act. Many of these grounds relate to default on
the tenant's part. Some others depend on the tenant having
been given advance notice from the start that the landlord
would want the property back in the future for some particular
purpose. One example would be where a property is let by an
owner-occupier while s/he is working abroad and that s/he will
want it back on her/his return.

The minimum notice period that the tenant is entitled to before
the landlord can issue court possession proceedings can vary.
There is no notice period at all where the claim is based on
allegations that the tenant has behaved in an antisocial way. In
most other tenant default cases, the period is two weeks. For all
other grounds, two months' notice must be given.

Summary of notice periods required:

- **Immediate notice**: ground 14 (antisocial behaviour,
  tenant causing a nuisance).

- **Two weeks' notice**: grounds 3 and 4 (holiday lets), 8,
  10 and 11 (rent arrears), 12 (other breaches of a tenancy
  agreement), 13 and 15 (wilful damage to the property),
  17 (making a false statement to obtain a tenancy).

* **Two months' notice**: grounds 1 (owner needs the property to live in again), 2 (mortgage lender needs to sell), 5 (property required again for a minister of religion), 6 (demolition or reconstruction), 7 (inherited tenancies), 9 (alternative accommodation available), 16 (accommodation linked to a job).

The notice in all these instances is a **Notice of Proceedings for Possession** and this must be on a specified form.

Landlord's right of termination

The landlord is entitled to end a tenancy agreement by entering the premises if:

* any instalment of the rent is not received in full within seven days of the due date (whether or not the landlord formally demands it)

* the tenant fails to comply with any of her/his obligations under the agreement

* the tenant becomes bankrupt or an interim receiver of her/his property is appointed

* the tenant (without making arrangements with the landlord or the landlord's agent) leaves the premises vacant or unoccupied.

The 17 grounds for possession which may be used as the basis for a possession claim are divided into two categories: **mandatory** and **discretionary grounds**.

Mandatory grounds

Once the landlord has proved that a mandatory ground has been made out, the court is obliged to grant a possession order. The judge must issue an immediate order that takes effect within a maximum of 14 days. In cases of exceptional hardship, this can be extended to an absolute maximum of six weeks.

Discretionary grounds

Where a discretionary ground has been established, the court has discretion whether to grant a possession order or not, or to make one but postpone its operation. In making this decision, the court can consider a wide range of factors such as:

* the financial position of the parties

* hardship to people living with either party

* length of time the tenant has lived in the property

* landlord's reasons for wanting to obtain possession

* health of the parties and their relatives

* age of the parties

* loss of amenities

* the public interest

* the conduct of the parties

* in rent arrears cases, the amount, history and rent direct arrangements.

(from Luba, J, Madge, N and McConnell, D, *Defending Possession Proceeding* 5th Edition, LAG, 2002).

When the court decides to make a possession order, it can order it to take effect at a future date eg in 28 days. Alternatively, it can make the possession order dependent on the tenant's future conduct, such as not to take effect provided the tenant makes regular payment of rent and pays a specified amount off any arrears. However, the order will then take instant effect if there is a subsequent default by the tenant. In that situation, the landlord is not required to seek any further court order.

Grounds involving rent

There are three grounds for possession involving the payment of rent. The existence of extensive rent arrears constitutes a mandatory ground for possession (ground 8). Extensive arrears are defined as at least eight weeks' rent arrears where rent is payable weekly or fortnightly and two months' where rent is payable monthly. This level of arrears must exist at the date when the notice of proceedings for possession is served on the tenant and also at the date of any subsequent court hearing. The reason for arrears is of no relevance to the court. It makes no difference whether the student is deliberately refusing to pay rent or simply awaiting a student loan or a cheque from an employer or parents.

If ground 8 cannot be made out, ground 10 can be used. This applies where there are arrears at the point when the notice of proceedings for possession was served and when the possession proceedings were begun. Ground 10 is a discretionary ground for possession. Making persistently delayed payment of rent is a separate discretionary ground (ground 11) and whether there are any arrears when the proceedings for possession are begun, is irrelevant.

If discretionary rent grounds are proved, the court can grant an outright possession order or grant one but postpone its operation. Such postponed possession orders are common in rent arrears cases. However, courts are sometimes less inclined to make postponed orders where arrears are substantial and when the landlord is a private individual. The order will be made subject to the tenant paying the current rent plus an amount off the arrears, unless it would cause exceptional hardship to the tenant or would otherwise be unreasonable. If the student breaks the conditions of the postponed possession order by missing one of the payments, the landlord can apply to the court to fix a date for possession. (The acceptance of further rent is unlikely to revive the tenancy – see *Burrows v Brent LBC* (1996) HL.) This procedure applies to all postponed possession orders made after 6 July 2006. If the student still does not comply with the terms of the order, the landlord may then ask the county court bailiff to evict them. This does not require any further court hearings.

Once the arrears are paid off, the suspended possession order comes to an end. If the student gets into further arrears, the landlord has to reissue the notice and re-apply for a new possession order.

Issues that are likely to affect the outcome of cases based on discretionary rent grounds include:

- Can the landlord's position be safeguarded by direct payments from the Department for Work and Pensions (where relevant)?

- Did the tenant have a good record of payment over a period of time?

- Did the arrears arise due to personal circumstances or wilful failure to pay?

Grounds involving default by the tenant (not involving rent)

There are four discretionary grounds for possession that focus on misbehaviour by tenants. Ground 14 covers the situation where the student's behaviour constitutes a nuisance or annoyance, or where the student has been using the accommodation for immoral or illegal purposes.

The nuisance or annoyance can affect not only people who live in the locality, but anyone visiting or 'otherwise engaging in a lawful activity' in the locality. While this clearly covers harassment of neighbours, it could also cover inconsiderate and persistent behaviour such as playing of loud music or blocking of entrances to the accommodation.

The immoral or illegal activity ground only applies where the tenant has been convicted of an offence that was committed in the locality, or that involves the rented accommodation. Typically, illegal activities can involve using the accommodation for selling drugs or stolen goods. Immoral activities are interpreted as referring to the use of accommodation for prostitution.

Causing wilful or negligent damage to the accommodation or ill-treating the furniture that has been provided can fall within grounds 13 and 15. An inventory attached to the tenancy agreement may be of some assistance, though most do not go into sufficient detail to avoid disputes.

Other breaches of the tenancy agreement not connected with rent can provide the basis for an eviction claim under ground 12. As this is a discretionary ground, not all breaches will lead to a court possession order. Hanging out washing in breach of a covenant not to 'hang on the outside of the premises any flower box, flowerpot or similar object, or any clothes, or other articles' is unlikely to lead to outright eviction, but it is conceivable that a postponed order could be made. Using the accommodation for business activities contrary to the terms of the agreement, would be regarded more seriously and could lead to eviction.

Where a notice is served making misbehaviour allegations, it is essential that legal advice is sought.

Grounds involving prior notice from the landlord

There are four mandatory grounds that are predicated on the landlord giving the tenant notice before the tenancy started that s/he would want the accommodation back at some time in the future. Even then, a court has the power to overlook a failure to give such a notice if it thinks it is fair to do so.

Ground 1 involves two possible scenarios. The first arises where the landlord had at some time occupied the accommodation as her/his only or principal home before the start of the tenancy. The second arises when the property is required as the only or principal home for the landlord and her/his spouse/civil partner, and the landlord did not buy the property with the tenants already living there.

Ground 3 can be particularly significant to students at colleges and universities in seaside or tourist towns and areas, as it allows landlords to let out holiday accommodation over the winter, and guarantees repossession when they want to let the accommodation during the summer to holiday-makers. It can be used where the winter let to the student is for a fixed term of not more than eight months, provided the accommodation has been occupied as a holiday letting at some time in the twelve months before the student's tenancy started.

Ground 4 allows universities and colleges to let out halls of residence over college vacation periods to tourists and holiday-makers, and be sure to get the property back for the next semester. It can be used to recover possession where the property is let to non-students for a fixed term of not more than twelve months, provided it has been occupied by students at some point within the previous twelve months.

Ground 5 applies where the accommodation has been let temporarily, but is now required as a residence for a minister of religion.

Ending a fixed-term letting early

Even where a fixed-term letting has not expired, it may be possible for the landlord to end the agreement and evict the student before the period expires. However, the Act restricts the number of grounds on which a court possession order can be obtained ie grounds 1, 3 to 7, 9 or 16 may not be used. A court will only make an order on any of the remaining grounds if the terms of the tenancy as written in the agreement make provision for it to be brought to an end on any of those grounds.

Suitable alternative accommodation

In some circumstances, a landlord may seek to move a tenant to alternative accommodation. If the tenant refuses to move, the landlord can try to get her/him evicted from the current accommodation via ground 9. As well as offering a comparable degree of security to the present accommodation, the new accommodation has to be 'reasonably suitable' as regards the rent, proximity to work, and the type and size of the accommodation (part III, Schedule 2, Housing Act 1988). Apart from the type of tenancy offered, this does not mean it necessarily has to be as suitable (or as pleasant) as the current accommodation.

Given that ground 9 is discretionary, the landlord must not only show that the alternative accommodation is suitable, but also that it is reasonable for the tenant to be evicted for refusing to accept it.

Where a case on ground 9 succeeds, the alternative accommodation must still be available after the possession order is made.

Substantial building works

Living in accommodation where building work is going on is likely to be disruptive for most students. However, ground 6 provides a mandatory ground that can result in a tenant being evicted where the landlord intends to demolish, reconstruct or carry out substantial work on the property. It is a complex ground, but ultimately, in order to stay, the student must be willing to allow access. S/he must also be prepared to move into another part of the property to allow the work to be done. Failure to do so could lead to eviction under ground 6. It should be noted that the landlord is not obliged to find the student any alternative accommodation following such an eviction.

Obtaining the tenancy by making a false statement

A landlord can seek possession where it transpires that the tenant made a false statement in order to get the accommodation (ground 17). A student who falsified references from a past landlord or a bank, could end up being evicted. However, it must be shown that the statement influenced the granting of the tenancy and that the tenant made the statement knowing it was false or reckless as to its truth.

Mortgage repossession

It is not uncommon for owner-occupiers who are having difficulty paying their mortgage to let out part or the whole of the property as a way of obtaining extra income. This means that the student can be very vulnerable as a tenant if the landlord subsequently defaults. In worse case scenarios, lenders have repossessed the property and evicted students without them having any idea what is going on. Ground 2, nevertheless, provides a mandatory ground for a landlord to evict a tenant where a mortgage lender requires vacant possession of the property to sell it.

Students facing eviction through mortgage default should ask the university or college accommodation service to negotiate with the mortgage lender. The mortgage lender may be prepared to let the property to the students after repossession, particularly if the housing market makes selling difficult.

Succeeding to a tenancy

A periodic assured tenancy, including a periodic assured shorthold tenancy, can be passed on after the death of the tenant, only to a partner who was living with them (married, civil partner or co-habitee). Different rules apply to fixed-term tenancies. If there is a possibility of any of the above applying to a student tenant they should seek legal advice.

Accommodation that comes with a job

If the student has accommodation that comes with a job, s/he could either be regarded as a licensee or a tenant. The student will be a licensee if it is reasonably necessary for her/him to live there in order to be able to perform the job. If the accommodation is not reasonably necessary, the student could be a tenant. However, if s/he loses or leaves the job, the landlord (and employer) can try to evict her/him using ground 16.

Registered social landlords (housing associations)

As mentioned in Chapter 2, housing associations are independent, non-profit making organisations whose function includes the provision of rented accommodation. Most, though not all, are categorised as **registered social landlords** (RSLs) through registration with the Tenants Services Authority (TSA) (formerly the Housing Corporation). RSLs use the same forms of letting as private landlords. However, very long-standing RSL tenants (whose tenancy started before 15 January 1989) have the same security as secure council tenants. As well as having their own rules, housing associations are also bound to comply with circulars and guidance issued by the TSA. These aim to ensure that in practice, housing associations act in a responsible manner. In particular, the TSA gives guidance in its regulatory code that legal repossession of a property should be sought as a last resort.

Some housing associations provide housing to colleges and the colleges let the accommodation to students. In this situation, the rules about college landlords apply.

Where a student rents directly from an RSL, it will be either on the basis of an **assured** or **assured shorthold tenancy**. The notice procedure and grounds for possession are similar to those applicable to the private landlord.

Rent arrears

In the past, some RSLs have commonly used ground 8 (the mandatory extensive arrears ground) when dealing with rent arrears. However, current good practice guidance issued by the Chartered Institute of Housing to housing associations discourages its use.

Domestic violence

An additional discretionary ground for possession is available to RSLs in some situations involving violence or threats of violence between co-habitees (ground 14A). This can apply where the accommodation is occupied by a married couple, or a couple living together as civil partners or as co-habitees. One or both of the partners must be a tenant, and one partner must have left because of violence or threats of violence by the other. The threats can be either towards that partner, or towards a member of that partner's family who was residing with the partner immediately before s/he left. The court must be satisfied that the partner who has left is unlikely to return.

When a student leaves 11

Subjects covered in this chapter include...

Bills

Money the tenant has spent on the accommodation

Recovering the tenant's deposit

Getting a reference from the landlord

Bills

Where there are sharers, utility bills may be in the name of one or more occupier. Where one occupier is a direct customer, they should make certain that they have made the necessary leaving arrangements with service providers, such as telephone, water, electricity and gas companies. This will ensure that their future liability comes to an end. Most of this can be done online or over the phone.

The occupiers should contact each supplier before leaving the property to:

- ensure they are aware that the occupiers are leaving

- give a forwarding address for final bills

- give a final meter reading

- terminate the contract.

A sharer with her/his name on an account who is leaving while others are staying, needs to ensure that the account is transferred out of their name.

Money the tenant has spent on the accommodation

Difficulties can sometimes arise where tenants have spent money on the accommodation and want to recover this when leaving. Where things are permanently attached to the fabric of a building, they can be regarded as becoming part of the building. As the landlord owns the building, the item becomes the property of the landlord and the tenant would not be allowed to remove it.

Decorating, or for example putting tiles round a kitchen sink or bath would certainly fall into this category – the tiles would be treated as a fixture and would effectively be regarded as a gift to the landlord. Doing work without the landlord's approval can lead to disputes. The tenant would not be entitled to be recompensed unless the landlord's agreement to the work had been obtained and agreement made about the landlord's financial contribution before any work was started. It is also worth bearing in mind that what a tenant might regard as an improvement, may not be viewed as such by the landlord.

Where things have been screwed to a wall, the situation may be more complicated. The general rules are that the physical degree of the fixture is significant – the more permanent the nature of the attachment, the more likely it is that the item has become part of the structure. Bathroom cabinets, overhead heaters and extractor fans have all been held to have become irremovable fixtures. Where there is a garden, cultivated trees and plants become part of the land. However, where something is attached, a more important question may be why it is attached.

While the courts have sometimes taken a more sympathetic approach to departing tenants, rather than to owners selling their properties, these can be very difficult issues to resolve. Tenants should be very cautious about attaching anything to rented property not least because the fixing may damage the property. The more difficult it is to remove an item without causing damage, the more likely it is to be a fixture.

The landlord might claim to be able to withhold the tenant's deposit to pay for restoring things to their original condition, and any dispute about this (see Chapter 3) might not be resolved in the tenant's favour.

Recovering the tenant's deposit

Disputes about deposits occur frequently when occupiers leave. Landlords can seek to offset any rent owing, unpaid bills, or damage caused to the premises, against a tenant's deposit. In its first year, one of the tenancy deposit protection schemes covering 200,000 deposits, had to deal with 341 disputes. In the most serious of these, the disputes were resolved with only 11 per cent resulting in the landlord retaining the full deposit. (See Chapter 3 for details of the Tenancy Deposit Protection Scheme.)

Where deposits are still outstanding from before the Tenancy Deposit Protection Scheme came into force (6 April 2007), disputes can still arise. A landlord may refuse to return the deposit or tenants may think that deductions made by a landlord are unreasonable. Ultimately action can be taken in the small claims court of the county court. The tenant's prospects of success are likely to depend on the evidence they can produce eg a receipt from when the deposit was paid. The tenancy agreement should indicate what, if any, deductions the landlord is entitled to take from the deposit. Ideally there should be an inventory listing the contents of the accommodation and its condition, decorative order and cleanliness.

As with any legal action, the tenant needs to take into account how much time and energy they are prepared to put into it. They should also bear in mind that it might be necessary to continue the process even after a court judgment where a stubborn landlord still does not return the deposit.

A common practical approach to recovering a tenant's deposit is simply to stop paying rent in advance of leaving. Of course, this is very likely to induce antagonism on the part of the landlord, as it will be a breach of the letting agreement.

Getting a reference from the landlord

One of the starting points for a new tenancy is likely to be a request by a landlord for a reference from a previous landlord. In particular, the landlord will want to check whether the tenant paid the rent regularly and behaved responsibly. While the previous landlord can be asked for a written reference, in reality, many landlords will wish to contact the previous landlord directly to verify the information. Landlords are not obliged to give references but if they do, they should ensure that they are factually correct and they should avoid giving unsupported personal opinions.

Useful contacts 12

Finding and renting out student accommodation

This list represents a small selection of the sites that exist and inclusion in this list does not indicate a recommendation. There are also many companies letting out their own accommodation which have not been included. For students, the place to start is the accommodation pages on the website of their university or college. Other helpful sites are:

www.accommodationforstudents.com (national)

www.homesforstudents.co.uk (national)

www.letonthenet.com (directory of letting agents)

www.outlet4homes.com (flat share service, national, gay and gay friendly)

www.lcos.org.uk (international students: London student hall and hostels directory)

www.studios92.com (short-term lets in London)

www.unite-students.co.uk (national)

Accommodation agencies

The Association of Residential Letting Agents (ARLA) is the professional and regulatory body for letting agents. It has rules and guidance that its members undertake to comply with so it might be worth checking whether an agency is a member. Unfortunately many are not. The website (www.arla.co.uk) enables you to search for local letting agents.

Advice and solicitors

Law centres, local Shelter advice centres, and citizens' advice bureaux can usually help with housing problems. To find local advice, help, and your nearest solicitor, visit the Community Legal Advice website at www.clsdirect.org.uk or the Law Society's website www.solicitors-online.com

Many universities offer free or cheap legal advice or help pursue legal claims, often run by law students under supervision.

Courts and legal proceedings

The Courts Service website (www.courtservice.gov.uk) provides useful information about how the courts work. It is the place to begin to find out about pursuing a small claim or possession action in the county court.

It is possible to make a small claim without legal advice or the help of a solicitor. The court service publishes a series of leaflets which explains the procedure step by step. For more information, visit small claims online at www.moneyclaim.gov.uk Possession claim online is the Courts Service's online service for claimants and defendants which can be convenient for making, or responding to, certain types of possession claim. For more details, visit www.possessionclaim.gov.uk/pcol

Deposits

To find out more about the Tenants Deposit Scheme, visit the Communities and Local Government website at www.communities.gov.uk/housing/rentingandletting/ privaterenting/tenancydepositprotection

Electricity

National Inspection Council for Electrical Installation Contracting (NICEIC) runs approval schemes for contractors undertaking electrical work – see www.niceic.org.uk

Energy performance certificates

Since 1 October 2008, all new lettings in England and Wales are required to have an Energy Performance Certificate (EPC). An EPC looks like the label that can be found on white goods such as washing machines and fridges. The landlord has to obtain an EPC from an accredited Domestic Energy Assessor. There is a maximum £200 fine for non-compliance. For more details of the scheme visit www.hcrregister.com

Environmental Health Officers

Environmental Health Officers (EHOs) can help with accommodation that is in a bad state of repair and particularly if there is a health risk involved. They can be contacted through the local council. They are usually found in a separate Environmental Health Department but may be found in a consumer protection or similar department.

Fire safety

The Chartered Institute of Environmental Health, LACORS (Local Authorities' Coordinators of Regulatory Services) and the Chief Fire Officers Association have jointly published guidance for landlords and fire safety enforcement officers on how to ensure adequate fire safety in residential accommodation. It includes advice on how to carry out a fire safety risk assessment. The guidance can be downloaded at http://tinyurl.com/5neqnb

Furnishings and furniture

A Guide to the Furniture and Furnishings (Fire) (Safety) Regulations can be downloaded from www.berr.gov.uk/files/file24685.pdf

The Fire Safety Advice Centre also has useful information at www.firesafe.org.uk/html/Legislation/furnregs.htm

Gas safety

For details on how to manage gas appliances safely and what to do in an emergency, visit www.hse.gov.uk/gas/domestic

The site also provides advice for landlords, and letting agents on how to comply with the law. The leaflet *Gas appliances – get them checked, keep them safe* can be downloaded from www.hse.gov.uk/pubns/indg238.pdf

There is also a Gas Safety Advice Line 0800 300 363.

Shelter

Shelter has advice services around Britain, where students can get housing advice in person, and in many cases, also get help with care needs, disability rights and entitlements, and debt or welfare benefit problems. Call 0845 458 4590 to find the nearest one.

Shelter has a free housing advice helpline 0808 800 4444 (open seven days a week from 8am to 8pm; charges may apply to mobile phone calls).

Practical, detailed information on a range of housing issues is available on Shelter's website, as well as useful guides, checklists, and sample letters which can be downloaded. Visit www.shelter.org.uk/adviceonline

Tailored advice for 16- to 25-year-olds is available at www.shelter.org.uk/knowyourrights

Tenancy agreements

Unfair tenancy terms: don't get caught out, a useful leaflet about unfair tenancy terms can be downloaded at www.oft.gov.uk/shared_oft/consumer_leaflets/general/oft381.pdf

Tenancy Relations Officers

Tenancy Relations Officers (TROs) can assist tenants who are being harassed or have been illegally evicted by their landlord. Some also deal with accommodation agencies that make illegal charges. They can be found in council housing departments and sometimes in consumer protection departments. More information can be found on the Association of Tenancy Relations Officers' website, www.atro-online.com

Useful publications

Housing Rights Guide 2008-09, Geoffrey Randall, 2007 (Shelter) see www.shelter.org.uk/publications

Guide to Housing Benefit and Council Tax Benefit 2008-9, John Zebedee, Martin Ward and Sam Lister, 2008 (CIH/Shelter).

Student Support and Benefits Handbook: England, Wales and Northern Ireland 2008/09, 6th edition, 2008 (CPAG).

A Practical Approach to Housing Law, Graham Robson and David Roberts, 2005 (Cavendish Publishing).

Text and Materials on Housing Law, David Hughes, Martin Davis, Veronica Matthew and Alwyn Jones, 2005 (OUP).

Shelter produces a series of booklets that give practical, action-focused information and advice for people facing housing problems. Written in jargon-free language, they clearly outline people's rights and responsibilities. Titles in this series include: *Gas and fire safety, Getting repairs done, Finding a place to live, Housing benefit and local housing allowance, Rent arrears, Know your rights, Private tenancies, and Harassment and illegal eviction.* For more information, visit www.shelter.org.uk/guides

Index